HAUNTED ATLANTA & BEYOND

TRUE TALES OF THE SUPERNATURAL

WILLIAM N. BENDER

CURRAHEE BOOKS
Toccoa, Georgia

CURRAHEE BOOKS

138 N. Pond St.
Toccoa, Georgia 30577
800-991-1114
www.curraheebooks.com

Unless otherwise noted all photographs are courtesy of the author.

Photographs credited to "LOC" are published courtesy of the Library of Congress.

Cover and Text design by Brandi Goodson

Printed in the United States of America.

10 9 8 7 6 5 4 3 2 1

Second printing

TO RENET

"The dream of life is over,
   The light of love is gone,
O! who would be a rover
   On earth like me alone."
   —Richard Henry Wilde, *c.* 1820s

"Resurgens" ("Rising Again")
            —City of Atlanta motto

CONTENTS

INTRODUCTION:
SUSPENDED DISBELIEF

The darkening night was breezy, trees swayed over the oldest graves in the city, and the sounds of the distant highway seemed to recede in the distance. The wind hid the sliver of moon with each sweep of distant branches. I could hear the individual leaves as they brushed past each other in an orchestra of sound. An eerie presence seemed palpable—just out of sight or touch, but one could sense a presence here. . . .

As you may imagine of a writer of ghost stories, I love lines such as those above, and have always been intrigued by specters, ghosts, apparitions, manifestations, and other true and documented cases of the supernatural. Still, I've had to endure the questions from friends and colleagues: "Why write a book about ghosts?", "Have you ever seen a ghost?", "Do you believe in ghosts?"

Since the latter question was usually the first interest many of my friends demonstrated in this book, I should answer this question first: do I believe in ghosts?

The answer is yes. I have to affirm that I believe in totally in the reality of ghosts, specters, spirits, etc. Ghosts are real; they exist in some fashion, and can on occasion manifest themselves within the range of our senses. While I began this book as something of a skeptic, I am convinced based on this project and my many interviews with totally rational people—many of whom were almost apologetic to be telling me about their true encounter with a spirit—that ghosts are real phenomena. Furthermore, these phenomena are worthy of our attention. While I am not sure exactly what a ghost is, I lean toward the traditional interpretation that ghosts are spirits of dead human beings who have somehow re-manifested themselves either in partial or in total human form.

If you, the reader, are skeptical, I'd recommend a position which I refer to as "suspended disbelief." While you may have difficulty in believing in each and every ghost story you hear (I do! Indeed, I suspect many manifestations or sightings are merely mistaken interpretations of normal events, while others are merely folktales), perhaps you can suspend your disbelief in ghosts when confronted with a series of otherwise unexplainable apparitions, situations, noises, or other circumstances that would appear to represent a ghostly manifestation. In short, I am presently prepared to suspend my disbelief in ghosts, and when I examine the stories and experiences of so many people—people who have seen ghostly manifestations in Atlanta and beyond—I am convinced that there is some unexplained phenomenon here which our species has yet to decipher.

Personally, I've never experienced a ghost—other than as described in "The Ghost Tavern" herein—but as these stories attest, that doesn't mean other sensible persons haven't had such experiences. In fact, a popular source suggests one in four Americans do believe in ghosts, and sixty-six percent believe in extra sensory perception.

In order to achieve the mental flexibility of suspended disbelief, I need only remind myself that one hundred and fifty years ago, not a single soul in Atlanta would have believed in the possibility of commercially available electricity, telephones, radio waves, television, space travel, or indeed, in any flying aircraft at all. Only fifty-some years ago, spaceflight by man was virtually inconceivable for the average person, and landing on the moon merely a childish fiction—but, of course, that feat was accomplished in less than a generation.

Further, if our ancestors had difficulty believing in electricity only four or five generations ago, how much more difficulty would they have experienced if and when they detected the random power demonstrations of static electricity? In short, I think that there can be many unexplained phenomena that may represent life after death, perhaps manifested very infrequently and only momentarily. I can thus suspend my disbelief.

Now here are some things I *do* believe. First of all, I believe that it is quite difficult for anyone to really envision the future, and that the future may hold untold promise to—once and for all—explain the energy manifestations which have historically been known as ghosts. Next, I believe that energy is never lost, merely transformed.

With these beliefs stated, I am willing to postulate that perhaps ghosts may be some random form of physic energy from individuals who have died, and that within the next thirty to fifty years, we will demonstrate what forms that energy may take. Perhaps some form of human consciousness may exist independent of any human body which supports it. Consciousness may be some barely measurable electromagnetic effect, manifested only as a by-product of a living brain, but possibly reproduced by some willful mental effort only occasionally, after the supporting body and brain is gone.

This was, after all, the basis of the successful Central Intelligence Agency experimentation into the applications of "remote viewing" during the spy games with the Soviet Union in the 1970s and 1980s. One subject demonstrated a physical jump of human consciousness into a location in the Soviet Union when the supporting human body was in the United States. In those government experiments—funded, of course, by your tax dollars—this remote viewer was able to draw pictures of filing cabinets and other data storage locations, complete with the labels on the super-secret filing cabinet drawers. Only after the demise of the Soviet Union many years later were those cabinets located and the labels shown to have been accurately drawn.

Another remote viewer described the interior of a room in which an American hostage was being held in Lebanon prior to the prisoner's recapture by American forces. This type of intelligence information can be critical, but authorities at that time did not have any sense of the accuracy of that information prior to the retaking of the hostage. Still, these examples certainly represent some remote viewing ability or consciousness independent of a distant human body.

If I can believe that human consciousness can, on occasion, become uncoupled from the human body supporting it, then I can accept that perhaps said consciousness can, on occasion, reconstitute itself after the death of the body. Perhaps the occasional reconstitution (i.e., ghost) is in some sense accidental, and many ghosts *do* appear to be confused by their ghostly state. Perhaps the ghost does not exist between ghostly manifestations. That is, a ghost doesn't "go" anywhere unless he or she is doing a manifestation or haunting, and after the haunting, the ghost may simply cease to exist.

It would also be helpful to remind ourselves that, prior to the work of Sigmund Freud only eighty years ago, few people would have been aware of the existence of "consciousness." In fact, they also would have been unaware of realms of their own psyche beyond their conscious control. In short, for Civil War soldiers, cowboys of the nineteenth century, and even the early Victorians, the mind was exclusively the conscious mind, and no one believed in—or conceived of—any unconscious; indeed, no one believed in any unknown aspect of their psyche or character. Thus, only a few generations ago, the very concepts of the consciousness and unconscious mind were alien because the human experience did not include anything other than conscious experience.

Therefore, a ghost, in my view, is the "static electricity" of human consciousness occasionally manifested, when conditions are just right, and when some purposeful action on the part of the ghost wills itself into brief physical existence. As a result of documenting these stories, I am convinced that ghosts exist; if these stories as described here are not convincing to the reader, I can only attest that the process of researching, verifying, and interviewing witnesses regarding these unexplained phenomena was compelling for me. I have interviewed enough people, read enough believable accounts, and studied enough about ghosts that I am confident to state that, even without a scientific framework in which to explain these phenomena, *ghosts do exist*.

I should further state that, as a confirmed Christian, I considered the basis for ghosts in the Bible. I have found many indications that ghosts may exist (Jesus, the transformation, the Lazarus story, etc.), and further, I have found no biblical injunction which would seem to argue against the existence of spirits. I leave to others the contemplation of these stories in the context of other religious traditions.

For a more serious study of these possibilities, I'd recommend two books which I consider basic reading in this broad field of physic powers: Adam Smith's *Powers of Mind* and Robert Monroe's *Journeys Out of Body*. Each represents an exploration into human consciousness undertaken by reasonable, serious thinkers who I—as a reader who has suspended his disbelief—trust, and who can each provoke even the most ardent skeptic into new and novel possibilities. In particular, Monroe's documentation of his personal conscious journeys outside of his body does suggest that consciousness can exist outside the framework of the brain—at least under certain conditions. Isn't that what a ghost is? In short, suspended disbelief is a willingness to expose oneself to the possibility of ghosts—this is, today, my belief on the subject. From that position, the folklore which makes up the bulk of most ghost stories is quite interesting and in many cases, even compelling.

In the course of research for several of the early stories, another personal belief came into focus. I am certain that many of the people interviewed for these stories are completely convinced of the existence of ghosts. While most of the interviewees were not terribly frightened by their hauntings (though some very much were), each person has stated his or her story with conviction. Again, many were almost apologetic, in some sense, for having seen the ghost or spiritual manifestation. In short, people who I know to be completely sane and functional in their role in the world—most of whom freely admit that they didn't believe in ghosts prior to their experience—are relating stories of various manifestations from "cold spots" to "shadowy figures" to actual "apparitions." In short, I believe that *they* believe.

As such, the accounts of persons otherwise not predisposed to believe in ghosts is something I find interesting. This type of witness to ghostly manifestations is much more interesting that the starry-eyed follower of all things occult.

There are several investigative techniques I am not interested in for hunting spooks. As someone interested in ghostly apparitions, I find that I always want some insight into how a particular haunting has been researched and documented by the authors, but I am both disinclined, and admittedly too inexperienced, to use many of the suggested "scientific" approaches to ghost documentation. I'm not particularly talented with a camera and, as any competent computer user knows, photographs, including videography, are easy to fake. I have presented herein some "ghostly photographs," which the interviewees believed may represent ghosts, but I caution the reader on the interpretation of these. Also, I am not interested in the use of heat detectors, magnetic field detectors, or electromagnetic detectors, which may document the temperature differences or electromagnetic field differences which sometimes seem to be associated with ghosts.

Rather, I am extremely interested in the experiences of normally sane and sensible people when they believe they have seen or otherwise experienced the antics of a ghost. With this in mind, I do think it critical for authors of stories such as these to state who they talked to, what they themselves have seen, and what they did to investigate the haunting, as well as legends borrowed from other ghost hunters and/or writers. I find that most "ghost story" books don't do that; most such books merely retell the story with no investigative techniques mentioned, and no mention of who was interviewed. I am dissatisfied with that type of book and wanted to do something more than that here. At a minimum,

I want to present as much as can be learned about a ghostly experience, going cradle to grave, if possible, as well as how I researched the story. I want to play with interesting questions such as what makes a ghost, do they travel or manifest in different places, etc. Also, I want to put the ghosts in as much historical context as possible.

There is one additional reason I choose to study ghosts, and that is a general sense that our technological society will, one day, leave us out in the cold. Of course, the benefits of technology are manifest and paramount in today's world, and many benefits will, no doubt, be noted in the future. Still, I suspect that the next great evolution of the human race will be based on the powers of the human mind, rather than on technology or our ability to manipulate the physical world—a *Childhood's End*-type evolution of mankind, as envisioned first by the great Arthur C. Clarke. Perhaps the next leap in human development will be manifested in something akin to "the sixth sense," "astral projection," or "psychokinesis." I have a sneaking suspicion that, if the nineteenth and twentieth centuries were the centuries of the industrial, the technological, and subsequently the information and digital revolutions, the twenty-first century will be the century of a revolution in consciousness. This began with the "decade of brain research" in the 1990s, involving studies of brain-based cognition. In short, consciousness will, at some future point, be the primary, if not the only, worthwhile study for the learned person.

While I have no evidence (in the scientific sense) for this belief, it is a strong hunch of mine that my grandkids, looking at our generation with the unforgiving clarity of hindsight, will view our scientific/technological approach to "knowing" as rather quaint or uninitiated, in the same sense that we currently view our grandparents' suspicion of the internet. Thus, I wanted to study ghosts to prepare myself for an unknown and unknowable future.

I invite you to join me in this initial quest; at the very least, these stories are quite interesting. More substantively, I can attest that these phenomenon are accurately presented, as these experiences were related to me.

Again, I believe in ghosts. For you, the reader, I can only recommend a philosophy of suspended disbelief. After all, a true thinker looks beyond. . . .

CIVIL WAR GHOSTS OF ATLANTA

The history of Atlanta is not as long as that of many other southern cities—Charleston, South Carolina; Savannah, Georgia; and New Orleans are examples that come to mind. Some suggest that as a result of the its relatively recent founding, the Phoenix City of the South may suffer from a distinct poverty of ghosts and spirits. Indeed, there do seem to be numerous spirits in these other older southern cities.

Still, the history of Atlanta is rich, with the young city playing a major role in the Civil War and the development of the New South in the 140 years since. I choose to begin this book with a series of spirits that are associated with the antebellum and Civil War periods in some fashion. While numerous stories in this book offered extensive interview and investigation possibilities, the ghosts reported on in most of this section did not offer such extensive possibilities. Still, these spirits do indicate the drama played out here on the national and international stage in July, 1864. While not intending to be a definitive history of these engagements, an outline of these battles will impact the reader's understanding of the ghosts they have spawned.

The Civil War ghosts of Atlanta are generally associated with the areas of the city in which the various battles and separate cavalry actions were fought. Having offered a defensive campaign in a long retreat from Tennessee during the spring of 1864, General Joe Johnson's highly capable and seasoned Army of Tennessee fought one major defensive battle at Kennesaw Mountain only twelve miles north of Atlanta's present-day perimeter highway, Interstate 285.

Over a period of less than a week—June 22 until June 28, 1864—over five thousand soldiers died in those rolling hills, and a number of hauntings are associated with the Kennesaw Mountain battlefield. Several stories are included here that reflect those dark days in Atlanta's history, including the ""Ghosts of the Kennesaw Line" and "Spirits of the Kennesaw House."

Subsequent to the Kennesaw Mountain battle, General William T. Sherman's Union army fought three major battles on land that is today within the boundaries of Interstate 285. The first of these was the Battle of Peachtree Creek, with the battle lines extending along what is now Collier Road, from Piedmont Hospital to the west for some three miles. While over 4,200 men, in both blue and grey, lost their lives there, few spirits are associated with this spot.

Next came the Battle of Atlanta, with its four-mile battle line extending southwest from the present-day location of the Carter Center to what is today Grant Park. This action took place on July 22, 1864, and over six thousand men died there. Presumably the spirits in Colonel Robert August Alston's 1856 house in East Lake, in Underground Atlanta, and in the Village Inn at Stone Mountain are all related to this battle. Of course, the many spirits which manifest themselves at Oakland Cemetery could have been associated with the Battle of Atlanta or any of these battles.

Finally, the Battle of Ezra Church took place to the southwest of the old city. Only one earthwork is extant from this battle, and that is currently located in Westview Cemetery. I found no spirits associated with the Battle of Ezra Church, though there are other ghosts in the area of Southwest Atlanta.

With this brief history as a background, here are the tales, and my investigations of them, to the degree that investigative possibilities offered themselves. Judge for yourselves the veracity of these spiritual manifestations from the most bloody war fought on our nation's soil.

GHOSTS OF THE KENNESAW LINE

The mist is heavy almost any spring morning on the northwest face of Kennesaw Mountain; the morning fog was thick when I arrived, the air sweet. The suburban sprawl that I had recently left behind on the country road seemed only a memory. As I turned off the engine and left the car, I heard a whippoorwill singing, lonely, in the distance; I knew what that song meant and I sensed pain in the mist all around me.

On a morning such as this, one can easily be convinced that this is a holy spot. Dripping in peaceful morning mist, it is not easy to envision the pain, the bodily dismemberment, the rage at the inconsequential deaths that plagued this unassuming hill in the declining years of the Civil War, the summer of 1864.

Here, on this ground, 160,000 Americans fought each other; 60,000 in gray or "butternut" (a yellow/gray homespun in which the Confederates were clad by that time) versus 100,000 in blue. They fought and died here by the thousands. This is the scene of an uncharacteristic battle—a direct frontal assault, blue on gray. Dangerous, bloody, and deadly; it was a confrontation of epic proportions, with thousands of men's lives in the balance. In such places ghosts abide and whippoorwills sing, forlorn in the distance.

On this battlefield, one can walk where the soldiers walked, see the earthworks on Pigeon Hill where hundreds died, contemplate the feelings of men facing the doom of the Dead Angle, or the beauty of the fields of Peter Valentine Kolb's 1836 farm. We can note the living observers to those battles of yesterday: the hickory and oak trees which, in their youth, were misshapen by the flying miniballs and which today stand as curved freaks of nature, living evidence of flying lead and the instant death of the thousands of men on the rolling hills below. Native American legend holds that hearing a whippoorwill on the eve of battle is the harbinger of one's own death, and the diaries of the Confederates who fought here registered that belief. As I walked up the hill, I noted again that plaintive call. They abound on this field, heard by many in the morning mist. Still, there are the restless spirits here—the undead who relive forever this epic confrontation. They are the ghosts of the Kennesaw Line.

Union troops numbered one hundred thousand on the Kennesaw Line.

GHOSTS IN THE HALLWAY

One would not initially expect ghosts in the upscale suburban homes that now cover much of this landscape. Today, the Kolb farmhouse, located on the extreme western end of the Confederate defensive line at Kennesaw, has been restored to its Civil War appearance, and only a small plot of land near the farm is preserved within the Kennesaw Mountain National Battlefield. Most of the land around the farm has been developed and, as Atlanta and Marietta continue to grow, the battlefield areas outside the park are lost to what some call "progress." However, the spirits, by all accounts, pay little attention to the delicate refinements of urban development and merely go on their merry way, manifesting themselves along deserted roadsides within the park, or in the modern hallways, bedrooms, or kitchens which are now found on the spot where they died. Many residents in these subdivisions have reported strange occurrences that they believe to be manifestations of a ghostly nature.

The Georgia Haunt Hunt Team reports that a Mr. and Mrs. Tatum, as one example, purchased a piece of property just across from Kolb Farm, falling in love with the forested hills in the area. The two-story house has been the location for several specters and other manifestations which the Tatums assume to be soldiers who fought and died in this battle. One evening the Tatums went to use the bathroom; Mr. Tatum, getting out of bed first, went to the bathroom nearest their bedroom, while his wife used the second bathroom off the adjoining hallway. In a moment, Mrs. Tatum saw a shadowy figure of a man silently walk by her bathroom door, wearing a hat and a long overcoat of the Civil War era and swinging his arms as he walked. The man continued down the dark stairs, disappearing from sight. Mrs. Tatum, trying to make sense of this apparition, at first thought her husband had, for some reason gone downstairs, but subsequently found him back in bed in the upstairs bedroom!

There were numerous other haunting experiences in the Tatum household. Mrs. Tatum reported a "cold spot" which she has felt numerous times in the upstairs hallway and in one of the upstairs guestrooms. Once, while putting a dish in the microwave oven, she felt something tug twice on her blouse. Upon turning around, she found that no one was there; her husband was outside at the time. On another occasion, Mrs. Tatum was reading after dinner and heard an electric drill in the hallway, turning on and off repeatedly. Mr. Tatum had used the drill that day to fix the floor in the hallway, but was not using it that night. When she investigated, she found the drill off and cold to the touch. Mr. Tatum had not used it that evening, and no one else was in the house.

As a final example, the Tatums kept a small bell in an upstairs room, which Mrs. Tatum would ring if she wanted her husband to come upstairs to assist with something. The apparition began to ring the bell on occasion, and when Mr. Tatum went upstairs, the bell would stop ringing. Each time Mrs. Tatum confirmed that she had not rung the bell, but once when Mr. Tatum began to go downstairs, it began to ring again! The couple developed a signal—Mrs. Tatum agreed to ring the bell only three times when she wanted her husband's help upstairs, and thus Mr. Tatum would know it was she who had rung the bell. Unfortunately, the ghost apparently listened to the plan, because the bell was soon heard to ring three times. Mr. Tatum answered by going upstairs, and found that, again, Mrs. Tatum had not rung the bell. Mr. Tatum finally announced that he would no longer answer the bell—and the ringing stopped altogether. Clearly the spirit in this spot is restless, and apparently something of a prankster—but why are there spirits in this modern neighborhood at all?

DEFENDING THE KENNESAW LINE

The Confederacy was defeated by the summer of 1864, but didn't realize it. The epic turning points of Gettysburg and Vicksburg had been lost by the boys in gray in the summer of 1863. Gettysburg took the aggressive spirit out of the Confederate army, while Vicksburg split the South along the Mis-

William Tecumseh Sherman and his troops rested at Federal Fort No. 7 September—November 1864 before continuing their March to the Sea. *LOC*

sissippi River. Months later, William Tecumseh Sherman began his Atlanta Campaign, moving from Chattanooga, Tennessee, towards Atlanta in a series of fights. The railroad city of Atlanta, the heartland and breadbasket of the South, the jugular of the Confederate States, was threatened by a hundred thousand battle-hardened troops in blue. Sherman famously announced that "war is hell" and, in his Atlanta Campaign and subsequent March to the Sea, his army proved it.

Sherman's early moves were quite straightforward. Atlanta was the rail center of the South, and thus was critically important for the Confederate war effort. Sherman knew this, and followed one of the rail lines—the tracks of the Western & Atlanta—from Tennessee southeast to Atlanta. Whenever the Confederate army under General Joseph Eggleston Johnston would set a defensive line, Sherman would use his larger, better-equipped army and easily outflank it, moving his men around Confederate defensive positions in Resaca, Adairsville, New Hope Church, Allatoona Pass, and many smaller battles or skirmishes. As Sherman approached the five-mile defensive line at Kennesaw, he initially tried to outflank this line to the west, as he had done several times previously. On June 19, 20, and 21, Union forces probed the line on the mountain for

Carte de visite of Confederate General Joseph Eggleston Johnston. *LOC*

weaknesses, but had not assaulted the strong defensive positions directly. Several days' rain had flooded the creeks which guard the approaches to the mountain from the northwest, and even the better-equipped Union cavalry had difficulty moving in the muddy conditions. Fearing such a flanking tactic again, Johnson moved eleven thousand Confederate troops under General John Bell Hood from the east end of the line to the west end on June 21, setting the stage for the Battle of Kolb's Farm on June 22.

Johnston could not have picked a more aggressive southern commander for this action than Hood: as soon as Hood sensed the threat, he launched eleven thousand Confederate veterans across the fields of a small farm belonging to Peter Valentine Kolb, without obtaining, or even seeking, the permission of his commander. Hood hoped to catch the Union troops unawares. Unfortunately, several Confederates had been captured previously and, under questioning, identified themselves as members of Hood's Corps. Of course, Hood's reputation for aggressive attack was well known, particularly by his friend and West Point roommate, General John M. Schofield. Schofield's Union troops faced Hood across the fields of Kolb's Farm. Thus, when Hood launched what he hoped was a surprise attack, with a desire to outflank the federal positions to the

On the land surrounding Peter Valentine Kolb's farmhouse, 1,350 men died on June 22, 1864. *LOC*

west, Union forces were well dug in and more than ready. The attack was an unexpected suicide.

Attacking to the northeast from just to the south of the actual farmhouse, across Powder Springs Road (the same Powder Springs Road as exists today), the Confederates under Hood raised the fearsome rebel yell and attacked repeatedly, even under the enfilade of northern troops. The miniballs and grapeshot (thousands of small balls fired as a single shot from a smoothbore cannon) tore ragged holes in the forward Confederate lines, but after a brief respite, the boys in butternut again raised their famous yell and came again and again at the Union lines.

The firearms and other battlefield weapons of this era maimed the body much more than the weapons of today. Grapeshot turned a mass of human bodies into nothing more than a bloody red mist in a fraction of a second; most often, no limbs or other recognizable body parts were left. One may only wonder about the soul of a man whose body has ceased to exist in the flicker of an instant— were these brave men even aware they were dying?

The bloody Confederate assault at Kolb's Farm failed—with Confederate troops reaching to within thirty-five yards of the northern lines but not dislodging their enemy. Stevenson's division under Hood was totally decimated, losing 870 of its 1,000 soliders on the field that day—the field which today holds the Tatum home and many others. Is there any wonder ghosts are about?

The wounded quickly overwhelmed the Confederate hospitals in nearby Marietta, and many were treated in the town square—the only place available to place so many dying men. After dark, these brave defeated Confederates fell back to their start point, believing they accomplished nothing. In fact, they had extended their defensive positions to the full extent of eleven miles, and their determined attack may have lead Sherman to believe he had already beaten the bulk of the Confederate army, thus leading to his decision for the frontal assault on the entire Confederate line five days later.

SPIRITS IN THE FIELD

Marietta resident Dan Cox doesn't profess any belief in ghosts, though he has had several unusual experiences which seem to defy understanding. Like many, Cox finds the quiet moments on the battlefield quite moving. He and I discussed the contemplation which this battlefield calls forth in so many—the beauty of the forests and the earthworks that witnessed so much blood

A Civil War re-enactor in Union uniform faces Kennesaw Mountain.

and carnage that now offer the opportunity for quiet reflection on life and human conflict.

Cox is the executive director of the Marietta Museum of History, and has had several ghostly experiences, another of which is related later in this book. While driving through the battlefield on Old Dixie Highway late one evening, Cox turned from a side road and caught a glimpse of a Union soldier in an open area near a railroad bridge. As Cox's headlights turned across the battlefield, he briefly saw the soldier with his musket, facing the mountain and the Confederate lines of yesteryear.

"I could see that guy," Cox says, "with that musket on his shoulder, standing right next to a tree just as plain as day."

This apparition manifested in what would have been the northeast end of the Union line, facing the Confederate line higher up on the hill. This Union soldier was spotted exactly where the federal troops would have been 160 years previously. This sighting occurred just north of where the visitor center stands today. Spirits also have been noted by many all along the Kennesaw line in numerous other examples.

WHY ATTACK THE KENNESAW LINE?

A direct frontal assault on well-defended and elevated positions—such as the Confederate line at Kennesaw Mountain—was a bloody affair. This battle strategy eats men's bodies by the thousands, chewing up whole divisions, corps, armies in only minutes. Desperate men rushing forward into the face of an entrenched enemy, seeing the smiles on the enemy faces in the breastworks, just before their own bodies were reduced to nothingness by fire and cannon; no other battle tactic of this era was as likely to result in the type of sudden, violent death which has come to be associated with ghosts. We have to ask the question, why did Sherman decide to attack in this way?

In the campaign from Chattanooga to Atlanta, Sherman's larger Union army outflanked Johnston's Confederate force many times, making for a rolling series of conflicts and fluid battlelines. Why would Sherman launch such a bloody, costly frontal assault on Kennesaw Mountain? Any of the earlier battle locations in the Atlanta Campaign—Resaca, Adairsville, New Hope Church, Allatoona Pass—would have been preferable for a frontal assault, with the terrain more advantageous for the attacker than a frontal assault on this mountain at Kennesaw. Of course, with a large force (one hundred thousand) at his disposal, and knowing that Johnston's force was much smaller, a frontal assault would have been one option for a commander to consider; indeed, it would have been a natural choice for a "hell on wheels" commander such as Sherman. Still, never once in all of May or early June of 1864 did Sherman decide on a frontal assault on any defensive position with the bulk of his army. Rather, he conserved his troops in each instance, using mobility to flank his enemy, thus forcing Johnston into defensive positions progressively closer to Atlanta.

Why then, did a frontal assault occur at Kennesaw? Perhaps the heavy rains on June 19 and 20 played a part, forcing Sherman to consider his limited mobility in such weather conditions. Perhaps Hood's earlier attack on the Union lines at Kolb's Farm played a factor—Sherman may have believed that he had broken the back of the Confederate force already. Perhaps Sherman merely wanted to test the mettle of the Confederates prior to engaging in battles in Atlanta itself. At any rate, Sherman made the fateful decision; the attack came on June 27, 1864.

"HELL BROKE LOOSE, JUST NORTH OF MARIETTA, ALL ALONG THE KENNESAW LINE"

According to Confederate diaries of the time, the whippoorwill sang in earnest that morning, and a brilliant sun rose, heating up that cursed mid-summer day. Union troops first launched diversionary attacks on both the east and west ends of the eleven-mile line, then Sherman stacked the bulk of his forces into two main attacks on the center of the Confederate defensive positions: Cheatham Hill and Pigeon Hill. Everyone knew thousands would perish in the hell of that battle, but such is the nature war.

The struggle on Pigeon Hill was a slaughter. This hill is no more than a small outcropping that juts out from the northwest corner of Little Kennesaw Mountain on the western center of the Confederate line. The battle there raged for two hours, with Union forces advancing repeatedly, only to be repulsed by concentrated enemy fire. The Union lost 850 men in a number of heated engagements, but never once were the Confederate defensive positions breached. The Union troops fell back, leaving the wounded and dying men to their fate on the steep slopes of Pigeon Hill, their cries of agony unheeded by either their comrades or their tormentors up the hill. Many bled out; others died of shock, wounds, and heatstroke. The sun was pitiless.

This hill is now preserved within the battlefield park boundary. In walking up a short hiking trail, I passed numerous Confederate rifle pits and earthworks, and the steep angle of the climb could only compound the problems of these attackers—it is a wonder any Union soldier who made that climb in the face of determined rifle fire survived. Many did not, and some, by numerous witness accounts, are still here.

DEAD ANGLE

The carnage at Cheatham Hill was even worse. On this central part of the field, the Union army actually faced east, across a small valley and creek. The Confederate positions conformed to the hilltop across the valley and turned at a sharp angle from south to southeast—that odd corner in the defensive positions was the focal point of the both the Union offensive and the Confederate defensive positions. Sherman threw eight thousand men against that angle. Division after division came forward, many in battle ranks, some marching upright in regimental columns; the concentrated Confederate rifle fire and the few Confederate cannon played hell with the men in these tight ranks. By the thousands they died, many at the foot of the southern breastworks—the dead piled high around the wounded at this horrid angle of hell, and many a Union man found cover behind bodies that only moments before had been comrades.

Reports filtered back to Union generals: "many wounded and dead" . . . "enemy works strong" . . . "heavy continuous fire" . . . "General Harker down." Clearly, even the generals behind the lines knew the situation was desperate, so they sent in the additional divisions that were initially to be held out of battle as reinforcements. McCook's Missouri brigade topped the Confederate works at one point in the struggle, and a face-to-face battle ensued—the most horrible of confrontations in this distant era of war. Men shot their guns into enemy faces two feet away and then swung their empty rifles like clubs, stabbing with bayonets and knives. Some threw rocks at the enemy, having lost all other weapons.

The situation was critical, and just as brigade commander General McCook topped the breastworks, he was killed. His subordinate, Colonel Oscar Harmon, probably never knew that he had succeeded to command—he fell within five minutes a short way down the line. Union troops were winded after their long charge across the fields, and the Confederate line held—with the troops in blue falling back to a slight rise only thirty paces from the front of the Confederate position. Here, by common consent, half of the Union troops kept up a sustained, suppressive fire towards the Confederate line while their comrades became moles—digging with everything within reach—bayonets, canteens, spoons, determined to scrape against the very earth until some cover from the deadly rifle fire above could be found. Rifle pits only inches deep, coupled with the slight rise in the ground, saved many a man's life that day; at night each side brought up digging tools to deepen their rifle pits. By morning the lines were only fifty feet apart, and each side held something resembling proper defensive trenches.

Here the attack ended in stalemate, and the armies remained for five days. Soldiers across the lines were virtually eyeball to eyeball—a phenomenon painful enough in any war, and particularly devastating in this confrontation. The wounded and dead began to stink and in two days a truce was called to remove them from the disputed ground, but never again did a frontal assault occur on this hillside. The gods of war had been appeased.

A short walk from the battlefield parking lot brings one to this angle in the Confederate earthworks, and we owe a moment's pause for reflection to the ones who died here. As I stood at Dead Angle, birds fluttered in trees which were only sprouts during the battle. I heard again the whippoorwill in the distance; I was listening then for that plaintive call. The few other visitors to the battlefield that day spoke in whispers, preferring to hear the wind in the trees and the birds singing. An unknown Confederate soldier is buried just a few feet from Dead Angle; the spirits here are vividly real and one can sense their presence. The Dead Angle is well named. The most ardent skeptic can become a believer in ghosts here.

Within days, the Confederates were flanked to the west again and were forced to withdraw from the field at Kennesaw Mountain. In just under two weeks, four thousand men had died on the Kennesaw Line; three thousand were men in blue. This is a relatively small number when compared to the massive battles in northern Virginia, but it is enough to leave some spirits behind. The Union troops in short order moved into Marietta beyond the mountain, and the Kennesaw Line was no more.

LEAVING ONLY THE SPIRITS

Only the spirits remain in this most holy of forests. The courage, the blood, the grapeshot are all gone; the mounded earth, worn down by time and the elements, exists to mark the defensive lines of death and sacrifice. Some of the trees, misshapen by the battle, stand guard over the battlefield and the spirits of the dead below; the whippoorwill cries his lonely refrain, announcing for all eternity the deaths of so many.

What does it mean for one's body to disintegrate within an instant? It must seem almost like an explosion from within. Does consciousness survive for a brief time, or perhaps for a longer time? Many ghosts seem to be associated with violent, unexpected, and sudden deaths. Does the soul survive for over 140 years on such hallowed death ground as this? How can the deaths of so many, in such a desperate struggle be understood? Most important, how should we, today, reflect on this ground where American fought American, where so many died, giving everything they had? Do we owe them some measure of eternal peace and, if so, how can these restless spirits be atoned?

Perhaps respect for their sacrifice, both blue and gray, is the answer. I urge each visitor to drive these country roads at dusk, spend time with the dead at Dead Angle or Pigeon Hill, listen to the whippoorwills, and sense the desperation of men facing their own death on these fields. Imagine the smells, the sounds, the intensity of the desperate battle here. Drive through when the evening sun is casting yellow and red light on this field, and look across these fields of honor. Better yet, walk the trails in the morning mist, the air redolent with the existential promise of these ghosts. You can sense their presence. Look quickly at the turn in the road, past the highway, to the edge of the field, into the earthworks. Here you are likely to see him, the lone soldier—the soldier who died not knowing why, not understanding—listening for that dreaded song of the whippoorwill. Should you be fortunate, you will catch him unawares; if so, be respectful, wave slowly to him, wish him well. Here the spirits walk on the land they fought and died for. Here, the ghosts of the Kennesaw Line linger on.

COLONEL ALSTON'S GHOST
IN EAST LAKE

Tim awoke, terrified in the blackness, the middle of the night. Someone or some *thing* was sitting on his chest—he couldn't roll over, he couldn't move. He was sleeping in the northern upstairs room of his parents' newly purchased historic home on Alston Drive in the East Lake area of Atlanta. After some time, he found that he could roll over. However, when he did, he experienced the same phenomenon again: the weight of a man—or a ghost—pinned him to the bed. Tim had met, rather dramatically, the ghost of Alston Drive.

After this harrowing night ended, Tim absolutely refused to spend the night in either of the upstairs bedrooms again. In fact, he took a sleeping bag and stayed downstairs, not wanting the experience repeated. To this day, according to his parents, he refuses to go upstairs in the old house that his parents love.

When Sylvia and Charlie Harrison purchased the antebellum house, Charlie was not thrilled with the hours of work involved in planning and restoring an historic home, but Sylvia had always wanted to undertake such a project, and this house offered just such an opportunity. This is the second oldest house in Atlanta and one with a generous blessing of old southern charm. Neither suspected at that time that their new project came with a resident ghost.

The house had originally been built in 1856 by Colonel Robert August Alston on land which was then several miles to the southeast of the growing city of Atlanta. While the story of Col. Alston is a critically important component of Atlanta's nineteenth-century history, I was interested in the ghostly manifestations in the old house. Many different experiences serve to document this ghost and, in addition to historical research, I was able to interview Charlie and Sylvia at some length, but not their son. The Harrisons received me in their beautiful home and showed the graciousness only Atlanta natives can offer.

THE MOST HISTORIC HOUSE IN ATLANTA

Meadow Nook, the original name of this house, is a rare and lovely example of a pre-Civil War planter's house. While General Sherman's Atlanta Campaign destroyed many fine buildings, including almost all of the antebellum houses in downtown Atlanta, this structure was spared. It was used as a headquarters for General Schofield, a Union General of the Army of Ohio, during the Battle of Atlanta, in July of 1864. Located on the southwest side of the Civil War city, only a couple of miles from Decatur, the house was posi-

tioned just far enough from most of the fighting during that battle to be spared. In fact, at various times many Confederate and Union soldiers camped in the fields around the house on land that is now East Lake Golf Club.

The original one-and-a-half-story house has remained almost completely unmodified, making

Does the Alston House harbor the spirits of one or more ghosts?

it a rarity among historic structures of the antebellum period. The front porch faced the main road of the day, though today the side of the home faces Alston Drive across from East Lake Golf Club. The new owners have attached a kitchen in the back, as well as a master bedroom to the north, but did so in such as way as to leave the entire front and side facade intact. This house is truly an Atlanta treasure, even without one of the most active ghosts in the city.

A HELPFUL SPIRIT

Charlie and Sylvia bought the house in 1994 and worked on it for two years prior to moving in. The house had been rented out for years prior to that and spent some time in the early twentieth century vacant. In 1996, when Atlanta hosted the Olympic Games, the Harrisions moved into the house, and strange, haunting experiences began almost at once.

Sylvia remembers her first experience. She was cooking one afternoon for Charlie's daughter's birthday and needed a can of olives for the dinner salad. She had been through the cabinets all afternoon and knew she didn't have any olives. She went to the phone called her husband to ask him to pick up some olives on his way home.

"When I walked back down to the kitchen, a cabinet door opened and a can rolled out in the floor," Sylvia recalled. "It was black olives. It gives me chill bumps now; I just about died. That's the first thing that ever happened to me."

Sylvia and Charlie have found pictures upside down or moved into the middle of the floor, and then turned face down. Other pictures, these of Charlie's and Sylvia's granddaughters, have been turned to face the wall. On one occasion, a picture frame was broken. It always seems to be pictures of Charlie's and Sylvia's family that are moved. Apparently this spirit doesn't care for others sharing his home.

Various individuals report "feeling like I'm in a spider web" while sitting at the dining table, and Sylvia believes this to be some type of unexplained spiritual manifestation.

"Things would fall. Like, most times when things fall off the mantel," Sylvia continued, pointing to the fireplace in the front corner of the room, "they fall on the hearth. But things here would fall off the mantel into the middle of the room. Things would *project*."

In describing this type of "projecting," Sylvia clearly indicated that some force other than gravity was needed to get objects that distance across the room. Here we have a totally unexplained phenomenon, unless one's resident ghost is at play.

Charlie tells of several harrowing stories involving previous renters of the property. These were shared with Charlie by the former owner of the house. Several students from Georgia Tech were renting the home sometime in the 1970s. While several went out to dinner, one student remained home alone to study. During his work, a sock fell on his book. Thinking his roommates had returned and were playing with him, he called out, "Leave me alone, guys. I'm studying." When a search of the house revealed there was nobody there, his skin tingled. He had experienced the ghost of Alston Drive.

Charlie reported that yet another group of renters became terrified of the continued haunting in the house. In fact, they felt that they could not stay in the house; they chose to break their lease and move out.

Another strange occurrence, shared by Charlie, took place in 1994. A nurse was renting the house and was living with a large dog. The dog would sleep on the first floor, as protection for its mistress, while the young woman herself slept upstairs. On two occasions the nurse awoke to dishes breaking downstairs. The dog apparently became terrified, and rather than attack the spiritual intruder, the dog ran upstairs, soiled the floor, and then jumped into bed with the nurse. None of these behaviors were typical of the dog, and the nurse became quite uneasy living in the house; she subsequently moved out. Thus, the spiritual manifestations here have apparently chased several groups of tenants away over the years.

THE GHOST OF COL. ROBERT A. ALSTON

Who could this mysterious ghost be? There seem to be a number of possibilities. First, legend suggests that a Union soldier was actually killed in the house by a Confederate sharpshooter during the Battle of Atlanta in July 1864; perhaps this is the spirit that resides here. Even today the banisters bear the marks of rifle butts, imprinted there by Union troops who, by that point in the Civil War, were showing no respect for properties confiscated for use by Union officers.

Both Sylvia and Charlie believe this spirit to be that of the builder, Col. Robert Augustus Alston, a mover and shaker in pre-Civil War Georgia. He is worthy of historical study, even if his spirit isn't the resident ghost. Alston was a man of great integrity, steely fortitude, and unsurpassed courage. His hospitality was legendary, and such luminaries as Jefferson Davis (soon to be the one and only president of the Confederacy), and Alexander Stephens (the vice president of the Confederacy) were guests there, as later was Robert Toombs (the spirit believed to haunt the University of Georgia's Demosthenian Hall and the Toombs House in Athens; see related stories in this book), and U.S. President Grover Cleveland. Anyone who was anyone in antebellum Georgia graced these rooms, and received only the finest that southern tradition had to offer. The stables were filled with horses of the highest breeding, and the library, paintings, and furnishings were of suburb quality. Further, the house saw great decisions being made from the time of its construction in 1856 until the outbreak of the Civil War in 1861. With the political leadership shown by Alston, the hospitality which was the hallmark of his home continued until his death in 1879.

ALSTON'S CIVIL WAR SERVICE

In May 1862, Alston, though a gentleman in every sense of the term, enlisted in John Morgan's cavalry as a private. He moved up quickly, and by the summer of 1863, he had been promoted to colonel and was serving on General John Hunt Morgan's staff. As a Civil War leader, he was a member of the famed Morgan's Raiders, a Confederate cavalry troop that operated largely behind enemy lines in raids designed to destroy Union supplies and disrupt Union supply lines. Once, on a raid into Kentucky—a raid on which neither Morgan nor Alston were present—Morgan's troops engaged in the looting of private homes and businesses, as well as robbery of a bank, from which they absconded with eighty thousand dollars. At this point in the Civil War—though not for much longer—such behavior, even on the part of enemy raiders, was considered uncivilized by gentlemen. Alston began an investigation of the raid and brought formal charges with the Confederate War Department against Morgan.

At that point, Alston found his investigation blocked at every turn. Affidavits signed by men on the raid disappeared from his desk, and Alston found himself reassigned to other duties in Virginia. Witnesses to the raid were likewise scattered by new assignments to distant postings. Morgan himself had the grace to be shot and killed on a subsequent raid in Tennessee. This anecdote is relevant in this context because the story shows the measure of the man. Alston was of such character that he would expose himself to ridicule, personal criticism, and loss in political influence to report a wrongdoing on the part of his friend and superior—even a wrongdoing (as such things may be judged) against his enemies in time of war. Alston demonstrated such bravery and fortitude throughout his life.

A GRAVE IN THE GARDEN

Another alternative to this ghostly identity lurks in the garden; the unmarked grave there may offer an explanation to this haunting. This specter may be the spirit of a lone Confederate soldier who is buried here. The soldier's commemorative stone, laid many years after the war under the garden gazebo reads

> George Morgan Rikard
> Pvt. Alabama Calvary
> CSA
> Aug. 15, 1835–July 22, 1864

The gravestone for George Rikard, a private of the Alabama Cavalry, Confederate States Army, and one historic letter tell the story of defeat and death in the Lost Cause. The exact location of his grave remains unknown. The marker commemorates a grave which has been documented in the letter as somewhere "near the southwest corner of the Col. Alston's garden." In the letter that initially surfaced in Ohio and was noted by the Granville Historical Society there, the death of Private Rikard was reported to his wife by his friend S. C. McCrary in July 1864 as follows:

> I am sorry to note to you the painful intelligence that your husband, George M. Rikard, is dead. He was killed on the 22nd of this month

by the explosion of a bomb shell while making a charge. Said explosion inflicted two wounds at the same time, on in the head, and one in the bowels. He died in about six hours after receiving the wounds. He was helped off the battlefield by my cousin, George S. McCrary.

I was not with him at the time he was shot, but as soon as I heard of his whereabouts I proceeded at once to where he was and stayed with him until he died, and buried him the next day two miles and a half south of Decatur at the residence of a Mr. Alston at the southwest corner of his garden, with his name, company, and regiment to which he belonged on the headboard.

The historic records are somewhat shaky on use of General Joseph Wheeler's Confederate cavalry during the Battle of Atlanta. Many thought Atlanta was already lost, and panic had set in on the evening of July 21, 1864. The action, now called the Battle of Atlanta, took place on the afternoon of July 22, 1964.

It is documented that General John Bell Hood, then in command of all Confederate forces, had ordered

CSA Private George Rikard's grave has not been located, but a marker is located near this gazebo. Does his spirit terrify the sleeping guests in the Alston House?

General Joseph Wheeler's cavalry to circle behind the Union lines and attack their supply trains at Decatur. This was to be coordinated with a frontal assault by other Confederate forces on the Union lines, which then stretched perpendicular to what is now Interstate 20 and reached all the way from the present Carter Center to near Grant Park in southeast Atlanta.

Almost all of the Alabama cavalry units would have been involved in that action, as most were under command of Wheeler, serving in a brigade commanded by Brig. General William Allen. Action in Decatur would have placed Rikard's personal sacrifice within two miles of Meadow Nook. Again, with no reason to note the death of one particular private (many thousands died that day on that two-mile battle line), this information may be all we will ever have.

Perhaps a spirit from Alabama roams these hallways, looking for something he knew in life before his untimely end, perhaps hoping to have his grave marked for posterity.

HONORING THE DEAD:
ADJUSTING TO THE SPIRITS

If the spirit of Rikard possessed such a desire for recognition, his wish was granted in 2001, some 137 years after his death. After considerable historical research, the descendents of George Morgan Rikard requested an opportunity to honor their ancestor. On Sunday, October 21, 2001, over one hundred family members gathered in the garden of Meadow Nook to pay respects to their ancestor buried there. They came from Alabama, Colorado, Florida, Georgia, South Carolina, and Michigan to honor their dead ancestor and place a grave marker in the gazebo.

Regardless of the identify of this spirit, the manifestation seems to be one of the most active in Atlanta. Pictures flying across rooms, people trapped in the upstairs bedroom, and helpful, somehow playful, antics such as the strangely materializing can of olives all suggest that this ghost is both real and quite active. The different experiences of the manifestations may suggest that several different spirits are active here. Some who experience these manifestations are terrified, while others are often helped by the spirits in this historic house. Though several renters have moved out because of this haunting, neither Charlie nor Sylvia seem at all frightened of the spirit. Confident that Col. Alston is the active spirit at Meadow Nook, and that he merely wishes to watch over his home, the Harrisons are quite content in their self-described role as caretakers of his lovely old house. Our best hope is that these spirits eventually find their peace, and that Atlanta grows to appreciate this architectural treasure and small piece of history.

THE HEADLESS SOLDIER
OF UNDERGROUND ATLANTA

With a wisp of wind over the tracks and only a hint of the noise of rustic cloth moving, you can hear him approaching. As you arrange your tools for the task ahead, you may glance over your shoulder in the dim electric light as he walks by, taking no notice of you. This spirit has no head, and in the dim dankness near the oldest rail lines in Underground Atlanta, with ground water lying undisturbed between the tracks, you see his reflection in the dampness. He passes you, recedes, and then fades to nothingness. You are terrified!

Such is the experience of the maintenance and security people who have seen the headless ghost of Underground Atlanta. Those who have encountered him say he merely walks the railroad tracks deep under the earth—never interacting with any witnesses, never noticing them. This restless spirit only walks when few are there to see him, this lone Confederate soldier—one of the thousands who died in or near this deep, dank place. Some say he is headless, others that he has found his head. But all agree that he wears the uniform of the Confederate

States that he died trying to protect. There are tales of many Confederate soldiers lying unburied here, and this one spirit watches their last resting place.

The soldier has been spotted numerous times over the years, almost exclusively by maintenance and security personnel; however, he has not been seen lately. According to Mary Jane Hearn, the guide and director of the Underground Atlanta Welcome Center, most of the sightings took place a number of years ago. All involved sightings that took place after midnight, and all manifestations took place on the lowest level of the three-story Underground Atlanta complex—in areas that are not accessible to the general public. No one knows for sure who this restless Confederate spirit may be, and few speculate. One thing is certain, however, in the old Civil War hospital on the corner of Pryor and Alabama streets—in what is now the heart of Underground Atlanta—thousands of Confederates died, perhaps scores of thousands. To those who study the spirits, it is no surprise at all that one or more of these lonely, distant spirits hang around here in the deep recesses of the earth.

Underground Atlanta is, today, a shopping and tourist complex with over one hundred stores, including everything from fine candies to sporting goods. A number of exquisite restaurants are found there, both quick-serve bistros and fine dining. Dante's Down the Hatch, one of the few businesses located on the lowest level of Underground where the original railroad tracks can still be seen, serves fondue and has a flair for historical decorations. It is on this level where the spirit of the lone soldier still walks after midnight.

A RAILROAD FOR THE CONFEDERACY

In 1838, construction began on the Western & Atlantic rail line between present-day Atlanta and Ross's Landing (now Chattanooga), Tennessee, over 120 miles to the northwest. Originally called Terminus, then Marthasville (after Martha Lumpkin, daughter of then-governor Wilson Lumpkin), and finally, Atlanta, our fair city exists because of this railroad. The early Irish workers lived in a rough-and-tumble town in the 1830s and 1840s, and worked on the new railroad. Each mile of the new rail line was marked with a mile marker, and the zero mile marker for this original railroad stretching into the Tennessee

In this 1853 map drawn by E. A. Vincent, the city limits are in a perfect circle one mile in every direction from the Zero Mile Post (allegedly the spot where Governor George Crawford [served 1843–1847] drove in the stake marking the terminus of the Western and Atlantic Railroad).

mountains from the south can still be found in the basement level of the historic Georgia Railroad Freight Depot next to Underground Atlanta. A bustling town of just over ten thousand soon grew up around the zero milepost on present-day Lower Alabama Street between Peachtree Street and Central Avenue. Atlanta was not the capital of Georgia then—merely the commercial center of the bustling state.

Later, as the Civil War loomed on the horizon, this rail hub was to become the central supply depot for the Confederacy. Even then, many suspected that war would soon come to this critical supply depot. But war did indeed come with a vengeance in 1864 when General William T. Sherman arrived with one hundred thousand Union soldiers and laid waste the city.

This three-part panorama taken from the dome of the Atlanta Female Institute shows Atlanta in October 1864. The city's commercial district is located toward the upper left horizon in the middle image; barely visible is the car shed passenger depot. *LOC*

THE CIVIL WAR HOSPITAL

Located on one corner of present-day Lower Alabama Street, where Dante's Down the Hatch now stands, a Civil War hospital once treated scores of thousands of wounded Confederate troops. (The well for the hospital, now covered with a brick safety covering, is located inside Dante's.)

Because of the rail connection, many soldiers from distant battlefields were transported there for their convalescence even during the first years of the war. Of course, when the war drew nearer to Atlanta in the spring of 1864, the hospital began to see patients whose conditions were much more critical, having just been removed from the nearby battlefields in north Georgia, Kennesaw Mountain, and Peachtree Creek.

In fact, those who have seen the film version of Margaret Mitchell's *Gone With the Wind* may recall a scene toward the end of the movie in which the city of Atlanta was being burned by General Sherman's Union Army. In that scene, a lone Confederate doctor is trying to tend the wounded at the hospital on Alabama Street with the rail depot in the background but the mass of wounded and dying men had overfilled the hospital and the men were lying unattended, on the unused railroad tracks just outside the building. Scores of thousands of

men died here—men from all over the Confederacy, in those critical days just before the fall of Atlanta in July 1864. Some of these men in the later days of the destruction of Atlanta lay unburied on the tracks long after death. That powerful scene in the movie depicts a horror that took place exactly where Underground Atlanta now stands.

While we have no exact knowledge who the headless ghost of Underground Atlanta may be, Hearn did indicate that the spirit is known to some as "Colonel C. J." We cannot but speculate that he is merely one of the lonely dying men who felt their life slip away while being treated at the hospital—or perhaps he died untreated, in excruciating pain on the distant railroad tracks, amid the smoke and carnage of a dying Confederacy, as the new and growing city of Atlanta burned to ashes.

This scene from hell witnessed the final moments of many young men—boys of fourteen, sixteen, or eighteen years, far from friends and family—who fought a losing war and then died alone on this spot. At least one spirit remains to seek recognition for that distant horror.

I talked with several other employees of Underground Atlanta, including a maintenance person and a welcome hostess. Those who had been around for some time all knew of the stories of the headless man, but none remembered any recent witnesses to the ghost. The witnesses are all now retired and unavailable. However, over the years, all seem to agree that this specter wears a Confederate uniform and that he walks only after midnight when the shopping areas above are deserted. We can only speculate on sightings which may have taken place between the Civil War era and the development of Underground Atlanta.

A DARKER HISTORY OF THIS LAND

In my research on Underground Atlanta, a darker chapter in the history of the south emerged, a history of the land the Underground Atlanta now occupies.

A sign over the storefront at 8 Whitehall Street, between Alabama and Hunter streets read

China Glass

QUEENSWARE

Auction & Negro Sales

The horrid history of slavery may be summed up in that bleak advertisement. The fact is that southern whites of the time considered slaves to represent merely another commodity to be advertised along with fancy glass and dishes for the dinner table, with such sales located right in the commercial center of town; today this view of human life is utterly incomprehensible.

There is an untold story here, a history of cruelty, and of spirits that should be here, but apparently aren't. I can't help but wonder why no there are no specters of Africans reported in this location. Of course, in retrospect, the slave market of the day was the one place that these human beings would be virtually assured of good food and reasonable treatment, since their owners would not want their "product" damaged prior to sale. It was on the smaller farms, and in particular the larger plantations of the Deep South that the horror of slavery was manifest. Perhaps we should expect no such tales in the old downtown.

Names change in time, as well as attitudes. Whitehall Street now holds the name of Peachtree Street in this locale, though Whitehall does continue south of this location. Hunter Street is now Martin Luther King Jr. Boulevard, and these name changes place the old address of 8 Whitehall, between Hunter and Alabama—right in the middle of what is now Underground Atlanta.

HOW IT BECAME UNDERGROUND

After the horrors of slavery and of Sherman's vengeance, the city grew again around the zero milepost. Given the economic disruption at the end of the war in 1865, many transients migrated to Atlanta looking for work, and the population of the city doubled to over twenty-two thousand by 1871. The Georgia Railroad Freight Depot—part of which stands today—was completed in 1869. Again the city grew, acquiring banks, hotels, saloons, meat-packing plants, law offices, and a whiskey distillery. Coca-Cola, the now-famous soft drink, was first developed and sold at the soda foundation at Jacob's Pharmacy on Peachtree Street. By 1900, the rail depot here was servicing over a hundred trains each day,

offering direct rail service, and connecting the far reaches of the southern states to such distant cities as Cincinnati and New York. Of course, with that volume of rail traffic, it became quite difficult to cross the street, and by 1910 several iron bridges had been constructed to cross the rail tracks at

The Georgia Railroad Freight Depot was built in 1869 and houses Atlanta's zero milepost.

Union Street on the second-floor level of the surrounding buildings. These evolved over time into concrete bridges with a mall on the higher level, along with a series of public plazas. During the 1920s, construction of these concrete viaducts elevated the entire street system by one level, and at that point all of the merchants moved their retail operations to the second floor, leaving the old first floors for storage and service—thus giving birth to Underground Atlanta.

The complex is now three floors deep, and the second, or middle, floor of Underground is now covered by the retail stores and plazas of the third floor. Most of the public doesn't realize that, as they stroll inside Underground by the historic markers and shops, they are on the second floor of the complex—an entire floor, generally unopened to the public, exists below the public level, and on that lowest level is where the headless ghost, Col. C. J., resides.

Given what this ghost has been through, I would like to learn more, and thereby show respect to this distant soldier from such a distant war. The sense of thousands of dying men, left unattended as that tragic war drew to a close, haunts all who know the history of this area, and a spirit with unresolved needs leaves me terribly unsatisfied. Perhaps with a bit more attention, perhaps after telling his tale more completely, this spirit, too, can eventually be laid to rest.

SPIRITS IN THE
KENNESAW HOUSE

A re there really seven hundred ghosts in the Kennesaw House? Who are these spirits? Is Dr. Wilder still performing surgery there on the Confederate and Union wounded from the Kennesaw battle lines only three miles away? Are other doctors here, as some accounts suggest? Are Dix and Louisa Fletcher still manifesting themselves from time to time to the numerous museum visitors? We know not who these spirits are, and we can only guess at how many men died in this old building, a building that served as a hospital for both the Confederate and Union armies during the battle of Kennesaw Mountain.

What makes the Kennesaw House so special? Why so many apparitions? There are so many manifestations herein, that it is one of the more famous ghost houses in the greater Atlanta area. This house has been featured on the History Channel's *Haunted Atlanta*, as well as in numerous stories on PBS, TBS, and most of the local television channels. Clearly, these are now some of the more famous spirits in Atlanta.

DR. WILDER APPEARS

Dan Cox is the executive director of the Marietta Museum of History, which is housed on the second and third floors of the Kennesaw House. He doesn't believe in ghosts, and insists that most of what people ascribe to ghosts in this building can easily be explained: an old building right beside a busy railroad track is bound to have unusual creaks and moans. Still, he does admit that some strange things here cannot be explained, and he recalls a newspaper headline that proclaimed that there were "700 Ghosts in the Kennesaw House." Perhaps he's seen a few of them.

The first strange thing that Cox can personally recall happened in 1992. Cox was overseeing the remodeling of the building at the time and noted that, on occasion, the elevator would come up from the ground floor by itself—the door would open and close and then just as quickly go back down again. No rational explanation has been found for the phenomena, and this strange manifestation continues to this day.

One evening in 1994, while Cox and his wife were standing by the elevator door on the second floor, he saw someone standing beside him. Cox started to giggle nervously, and his wife asked what he was laughing at. He told her that he'd seen—for only an instant—another gentleman standing right beside him next to the elevator door. The apparition was about five feet seven or eight inches tall. He had on a cream-colored overcoat or smock that came to mid thigh, and his pants were tucked into his calf-length boots. He had on a little flat hat, and Cox thought that the apparition's clothing resembled that of a Civil War surgeon. Of course, the apparition was gone "just like a flash of lightning." Two workers, besides Cox, have also witnessed this apparition of a man dressed as Mr. Cox described.

In later investigation, Cox confirmed that the building was used as both a hospital and a morgue by both Union and Confederate troops, so surgeons of that period would have performed their ghastly operations here, primitive by today's standards. It is probable that this building saw hundreds of wounded, thousands of amputations, and treatments of every kind.

Cox is a respected historian. He is one of the foremost authorities on this area of Georgia; he oversees in the collection of the MMH many artifacts and letters from the Civil War period. He has conducted research in a wide variety of

31

settings including the National Archives in Washington, D.C., and numerous families from the area have donated artifacts for the local museum. These credentials lend credence to his research and his descriptions of these experiences—he is a serious man, not prone to flights of fantasy, and he knows history well enough to know what would be expected of surgeons of that day.

Upon further digging into the past, Cox has confirmed that the Civil War-era owner of the hotel, Dix Fletcher, was a Union sympathizer, a fact that might explain why the building was spared the wrath of fire after federal forces moved into Marietta. Fletcher had a friend, a Dr. Wilder, who performed surgery in the hotel-cum-hospital during that period. Cox believes that this apparition by the elevator may be that of Dr. Wilder—still on his rounds in a hospital in which many soldiers, both Rebel and Yank, died. Dr. Wilder apparently has patients to tend and duties to perform that his spirit feels are unfinished.

HISTORY OF THE FLETCHER HOTEL

Cox, through continuing research, has amassed quite a bit of information on the old building. The four-story brick structure was originally constructed by John Glover in 1845 as a cotton warehouse, but around 1855, Dix and Louisa Fletcher bought the building and turned it into thirty-two room hotel. It was

known as the Fletcher Hotel through the first year of the Civil War, and came to be called the Kennesaw House only later.

Fletcher was a confirmed Unionist who came to Georgia from the north, first to Savannah, then to Atlanta. Because of his well-known Unionist sympathies, his hotel was one of only four major buildings in Marietta that were spared from Union fire. As was Union commander General William Tecumseh Sherman,

Many believe that Marietta's Kennesaw House—an 1845 cotton warehouse turned hotel which also served as a hospital during the Civil War—houses as many as seven hundred spirits.

Fletcher was a Mason; Sherman also left Marietta's Masonic Hall standing after the battle.

Finally, Fletcher's son-in-law, Henry Green Cole, served as a Union spy early in the war and was known to General Sherman as such. Cole obtained information from a black freeman who served as a barber to the Confederate officers, and then sent his intelligence forward to the Union leadership through contacts in Chattanooga, Tennessee.

With these numerous connections to the Fletcher family, the decision was made by the Union army to leave the Fletcher Hotel standing and use it as a hospital after the battle at Kennesaw Mountain. Cox reports that the top floor of the building burned in 1867, leaving the three-story structure which is preserved today. Earlier reports suggested that the Union army had attempted to destroy the building, but Cox's research has documented that the fourth floor was still there when federal forces left the area, and that later, the top floor accidentally caught fire and burned; it was the fourth floor which was used as a morgue.

Since the battle, the building has had many uses, including warehouse for rail cargo (the building sits beside the old depot), restaurant, and office building. Cox began to remodel the building in 1992 for his use as the Marietta Museum of History and as leased office space. According to Cheri Mohr Drake, a ghost hunter and leader of the Georgia Haunt Hunt Team, ghosts often become agitated when remodeling is in progress and begin to manifest themselves more frequently. Apparently, their environs become somewhat unfamiliar during remodeling, and this may be what took place in the Kennesaw House.

OTHER GHOSTLY MANIFESTATIONS

In interviewing Cox, I found his attitude of humorous skepticism towards these hauntings very refreshing. I interviewed a large number of people in preparation of this book, and I quickly discovered that I have more trust in those who indicate some healthy skepticism toward these phenomena.

Even with well-defined ghostly pictures of apparitions in hand from his security cameras, Cox toyed with the sunlight in the room where the pictures emerged and determined that these particular apparitions were nothing more than reflected sunlight. Thus, these phenomena are not described herein; they can be explained by natural means. Again, I find Cox's skepticism refreshing, also to some degree compelling, in that this witness has actively tried to explain away manifestations through natural means.

On one occasion, Cox heard a tapping sound from the stairwell at the southeast corner of the building. It sounded like a man tapping a wedding band or other ring on the metal handrail. Cox found this curious and left his office to investigate. He opened the door and looked down the stairwell, and finally went down to the first level only to find that no one was there. He returned to his office and heard the sound again. This time, Cox entered the stairwell, went down the stairs, and actually exited the building to see if someone were there— again no one was found. The tapping sound has never been explained, likewise this sound has never returned.

Cox once entered one of the rooms on the second floor and heard a woman's voice softly calling his first name, "Dan . . . Dan . . ." When I asked who that spirit might be, Cox insisted that it was a woman's voice, and thus not the voice of the mysterious Dr. Wilder. Perhaps it is the manifestation of Louisa Fletcher, the wife of hotel owner Dix Fletcher. Finally, Cox also reports ghostly happenings in his own office.

"My computer screen faces the door to the museum," he says, "and one evening a shadow went across my computer screen. Of course, the outside room was dark and when I looked around no one was there."

AN OPERATION AT THE KENNESAW HOUSE

Cox also reports that many spiritual mediums have told stories of apparitions in the building. Barbara Duffey, as one example, once experienced a brief apparition involving several ghosts. She reports that upon entering the second floor of the building, she saw an apparition of a surgical operation in progress. A tall man wearing suspenders and with his shirtsleeves rolled up was bending over a patient on a table. Several assistants were around, working frantically, and a short girl with her hair pulled back in a bun was holding a candle for light. The apparitions vanished as soon and as unexpectedly as they came. Duffey hurried over to the spot of the apparitions, towards the northwest corner of the second-floor room, but felt nothing further as she crossed the room or once she was on the spot.

It is interesting to note that Duffey had not talked to Cox at the time of this manifestation. Also, whereas Cox (who is over six feet tall) described Dr. Wilder as short, Duffey reports that the doctor in this surgical scene was "tall" and "brawny." Could this be a different view of Dr. Wilder, with Dr. Wilder seeming tall to a shorter woman, and short to Cox, or is this another spirit performing surgery? Presumably a number of surgeons worked in the Kennesaw House during 1864 and 1865, and the spirits of several surgeons may appear here.

THE SPIRITS TODAY

These spirits are still around; the elevator still has a mind of its own, and while Cox has not experienced anything recently, he indicates that each Halloween the local media have a feeding frenzy in his old building. Also, numerous mediums and ghost hunters have investigated this building. With his avowed love of history, Cox views this hoopla as one way to get youngsters interested in the numerous artifacts in the museum and the history behind them. Cox is always willing to spend time talking about the ghostly phenomenon that he can't explain as he guides tours of the concrete realities of history, the relics of bygone ages.

Spirits or not, the Marietta Museum of History is well worth a visit. You can see the hundreds of artifacts dating from earliest settlements in the area in the early 1800s through today and learn about Ten-Cent Bill, a slave who was a drummer in the Confederate army. Cox is interested in historic accuracy above all else, and his exhibits tell the true story of a period of great confusion, which only in retrospect, do we define into neat, easily understandable categories.

I was personally moved by an example of a Sherman's hairpin—sometimes called a Sherman's necktie—a section of railroad track heated over a fire of rail ties and bent by Sherman's troops to prohibit their use by the Confederacy. This metal survived because a newly freed slave stole it as a symbol of his new freedom—it stayed with his descendents for almost a hundred years. This reverence for a simple piece of bent metal moved me; for in the mind of a newly freed slave, this hairpin meant freedom to an entire race, and that is a historic sight well worth seeing, spirits or not.

ROLL CALL OF THE DEAD
AT OAKLAND CEMETERY

Many have reported hearing it—this roll call of the dead. Others merely shrug and suggest the entire tale is invented. Still, some quiet evenings, on the evening breeze near the unmarked grades of these Confederates who died in 1864, one can sometimes hear the names spoken softly, floating gently in the wind—a roll call of those who gave their lives for the Lost Cause.

The names are presumed to be those of some three thousand soldiers buried in several mass graves here. Many, though certainly not all, died nearby in the Battle of Atlanta in July of 1864. The battle lines came to with a couple of miles of the historic Oakland Cemetery. The best location to hear this spiritual roll call is near a prominent statute that serves as the only monument in the area of the unmarked graves, the "Lion of Atlanta." This beautiful marble lion represents the Confederate soldiers who died defending their beliefs. This artistic masterpiece captures the agony of the fall of Atlanta in 1864 and serves to mark the untold stories of men lost in that long-ago struggle. The proud, mortally wounded lion

At the Lion of Atlanta monument, one can hear the roll call of the dead, the names of the troubled souls of some three thousand soldiers who died in one of the last major battles for the Confederacy and who are buried in unmarked graves in Oakland Cemetery.

is lying down, signifying defeat in battle. In his paw, he clutches a fallen battle flag, and he seems to be pulling his beloved banner toward him. Standing on the summer grass beside the lion, one can almost sense the thousands of souls interred here and one may easily imagine hearing names, spoken by an unknown spirit, so softly. This place commands—and demands—reverence.

One only has to walk through Oakland Cemetery once to appreciate the beauty and serenity of this space—a location where the demands and expectations of the bustling cityscape of Atlanta, only a few feet away, seem quite distant and remote; a walk through Oakland is a walk back in time. It is well worth a summer afternoon stroll, spirits notwithstanding.

A SPIRIT'S CAR HORN?

Kevin Kuharic quite clearly loves Oakland Cemetery. He served as a volunteer gardener with the Oakland Historic Cemetery Foundation for several years before joining the paid staff there. It was clear from the outset that he revered the historic old cemetery and found an inner peace in his association with it.

After a day of gardening around an Oakland burial plot in 1989, Kuharic put his keys in his car ignition to begin his ride home and the car horn honked four times in rapid successsion by itself. That sent shivers down his spine, since there was no apparent cause for it and such a thing had never happened before. In fact, prior to that there had been no problems at all with the car, or the car horn, and there were no such instances afterward. Still, Kuharic thought this was quite strange, and for that reason, shared this "unexplained honking" with several friends. Over time, Kuharic came to view this as an isolated, though weird occurrence, with no explanation. "Several years later, I had a different vehicle. I came out to Oakland to show a friend around, and this person knew that story," Kuharic explains. "After we walked around Oakland, we got into this other car, put the key in its ignition, turned it on, and the horn in *that* car honked four times by itself. That was when I realized it was not just an isolated incident."

Kuharic has never understood the reason for four specific sounds, nor has any problem ever been found in either car horn. He clearly believes this to be a supernatural occurrence related to Oakland Cemetery.

Kuharic further reports that he believes in ghosts, and has had at least one "haunting" experience in Indiana. When he was living in a second-floor apartment, his neighbors reported several unusual experiences on the third floor of the building. Later, when he moved to an apartment on that floor, he experienced things moving across the room and flowers falling to the floor. He considers himself somehow "sensitive" to these haunting experiences, and while he suspects that others have had unusual experiences in Oakland, he could not suggest other experiences for me to investigate. Still, his haunting experience with these car horn blasts in Oakland will remain with him forever.

THE HISTORY OF OAKLAND CEMETERY

Oakland is a space of beauty and serenity in the heart of Atlanta. The present-day eighty-eight-acre municipal burial ground was founded as a smaller graveyard of some six acres in 1850. The cemetery served as the final resting place for nearly everyone who died in Atlanta from the 1850s through the early 1880s, including all races, religions, and social classes of Atlanta society, although in strictly segregated areas. Strolling though the older sections of the cemetery, one can find names of prominent citizens that, later in Atlanta's history, became the namesakes of well-known Atlanta streets, parks, and neighborhoods. Because these are the first settlers in this region, one gets a flavor for these early arrivals.

Buried within the black section of Oakland, one can find many leaders of the African-American community both old and new. Mary Combs, a freewoman well known in the Atlanta's antebellum black community, purchased some land on present-day Peachtree and Wheat streets in 1856, sold it for double in 1862, and used the proceeds to purchase her husband's freedom from slavery. James Tate, who co-founded the first black school in Atlanta, was buried there in 1897. Bishop Wesley John Gaines, a former slave and founder of Morris Brown College, was interred there in 1912.

In the Jewish section (the second oldest Jewish burying ground in Georgia) lay Dr. Joseph Jacobs, the pharmacist who introduced Coca-Cola in 1896, and Morris and Emanuel Rich, founders of one the largest retail chains in the South, Rich's Department Store.

As members of some of the city's most prominent families, novelist Margaret Mitchell and golfer Bobby Jones rest in the cemetery's oldest section.

The so-called Potter's Field is a four-acre area at the east end of the cemetery where Atlanta's indigent were buried in the simplest graves. At one time, wooden crosses marked the graves, but these are long gone. Now there is only one marker honoring all seventeen thousand people who rest here.

From a vantage point located in the present-day cemetery, Confederate General John Bell Hood watched the Battle of Atlanta in July, 1864. The Confederate section of Oakland, some twenty acres, resembles Arlington National Cemetery with its symmetrical rows of small, similar stones. It is the final resting place of much of Atlanta's Civil War dead. The uniform markers in this section, and the sixty-five-foot obelisk installed in 1874, mark the Confederate section of the cemetery. This central area inters nearly three thousand Confederate soldiers (including three generals—Gordon, Iverson, and Evans), as well as sixteen Union soldiers.

The cemetery not only holds graves, but history as well. Indeed, the rich history of all races, creeds, and classes is well represented within Oakland's walls. Clearly, this ground is both sacred and historic.

THE WANDERING SPIRIT

Jasper Newton Smith is one ghost said to haunt Oakland. Alexandria Egan reported on this haunting for *Points North* magazine in 2000. While I could find no witnesses to this reported specter, I choose to include it here as an example of some of the spiritual folklore associated with Oakland Cemetery.

Jasper died around 1918 and was buried near the entrance to Oakland Cemetery. Early in the Victorian era, Oakland had become known for its beautiful gardens, and quite often on Sunday afternoons, Atlanta's most prominent citizens would visit their family graves, frequently bringing picnic lunches. At the time, cemeteries were used as much as public parks as burying grounds.

Even in death, Jasper Newton Smith watches over Oakland Cemetery and, according to some, climbs down to roam through the graveyard at night.

With all of this activity in mind, Jasper left specific instructions concerning his mausoleum: he ordered a life-size granite statue of himself, resting comfortably in his favorite chair, be placed atop his grave, facing the entrance to the cemetery. He wanted to keep abreast, even after death, of the comings and goings at Oakland. It is said that at night, after the cemetery is closed to visitors, Smith climbs down from his prominent marker, and visits other spirits in the cemetery, watching carefully for any unusual goings-on.

Who can say if the spirit of Jasper Newton Smith comes down from atop his monument each evening to wander about the cemetery? Again, I could find no one to verify this story, but folklore of a spiritual nature abounds at Oakland.

THE ROLL CALL OF THE DEAD

It was a December afternoon when Norman Nawrocky visited Oakland Cemetery and heard the roll call of the dead, as reported by Nancy Roberts in her book *Georgia Ghosts*. In front of the Lion of Atlanta, Nawrocky, a student of history, considered the history of the destruction of Atlanta as Sherman destroyed this city on his "March to the Sea" during the last year of the Civil War. Nawrocky empathized with the utter despair of the civilian population of those distant times; he sensed the devastation that total war means to a civilian population. That is when he first heard the sound, gently on the wind . . .

"Abraham Alford," called in a harsh, authoritative voice.

"Heah," answered another voice, softly.

"Ira Allen."

"Here" was called in response.

Again the authoritative tone: *"Hiram Beard."*

"Here," returned a softer voice, like that of a wounded man.

One can only imagine the chills running along Nawrocky's spine as he listened to this roll call of the dead; not only the roll call, but the answers, varying in pitch and voice tone. These sounds came from the grave, the hallowed ground on which he stood. The calling of the list continued.

"Mark Davis."

"Here."

"Wilber Glover."

"Present."

"Herman Harber."

"Heah."

When one is terrified, one cannot imagine becoming more frightened. Still, as the roll call progressed, Nawrocky sensed increasing terror, and was then shocked to hear . . .

"Jim Nawrocky."

He didn't bother to answer as his own name was called in this chilling roll call; he fled the cemetery

A VISIT WITH THE SPIRITS

While Atlanta boasts many remarkable sights and highlights, every visitor—whether seeking spirits or not—should visit historic Oakland Cemetery. Here resides the most intriguing cross-section of the southern past one is likely to find anywhere—every culture, class, religion; slaves and millionaires; athletes and statesman.

At Oakland, one finds that the spirits somehow seem to linger, and just occasionally, their names are called for our eager ears to hear. Even if the legends are merely legends, unusual manifestations occur here with some regularity, and more importantly, there is a spirit of purpose here, to be sensed by those willing to take a few moments and open themselves to lessons from the grave. Perhaps some of our more important lessons can come from such places as this, and on sacred ground such as this, we should be prepared to listen.

GHOSTS OF THE VILLAGE INN

Scott and Lisa were married at the Village Inn in Stone Mountain, Georgia, just east of the Atlanta perimeter highway. The joyous occasion took place on a beautiful day in April 1997. The couple had invited many friends and family members to share their special day, but they were not anticipating any ghostly attendees. Still, the beautiful old inn—on the square in Stone Mountain Village, one block from downtown—has a mind, and perhaps a soul, of its own. After the other guests were gone, in the middle of the night, a ghostly visitor would show up.

Scott and Lisa had rented the entire Village Inn for their happy day and the wedding party went out to dinner after the ceremony. Soon after returning to the inn, the couple retired for the night. They were staying in the front corner room, the Blue Room, which according to legend, is one of the rooms used as a hospital for Confederate Soldiers in 1864 and 1865. Had the newlyweds known the lore, they could have anticipated some unwanted visitors! After their guests were gone, at around 3:30 A. M., Lisa and Scott were awakened by the door flying open and banging loudly against the wall! They knew that they were alone in the house because they had rented the entire house for their celebration. After a few moments, Lisa went to the door and shut it, and then went back to sleep. The next morning, as Lisa thought about the experience, she began to wonder more about it. She played a bit with the door, and realized that the door didn't latch well. Still she was convinced that, while the door would open slowly by itself, it would not open with enough force to bang against the wall. Neither Lisa nor Scott were aware, at that point, of rumors of ghosts in the inn, but Lisa was certain she had experienced something unusual that evening. They have also experienced a number of other strange events, including doors opening mysteriously or objects moving by themselves, and each time they stay in the house, according to Lisa, they experience some type of "presence."

HITORY OF THE INN

The oldest surviving house in Stone Mountain Village, the inn was originally built in the 1820s as an inn for the legions of visitors who came to enjoy the climb up Stone Mountain. The house has twelve rooms on three floors, and the

entire third floor—now one of the larger bedroom suites—was originally a ballroom used by the guests of the inn.

The granite peaks of Stone Mountain tower over the surrounding countryside by over a thousand feet and views from the top of the mountain are spectacular. The inn faces the mountain, with a

The Village Inn was used as a Confederate hospital in 1864 and 1865. The spirits of those who died here may still linger.

wonderful view of the granite dome, from both the front porch and the second story balcony on the front or east side of the building. By the 1840s, a railroad brought many visitors each year to the Stone Mountain for outings, and the inn would have been a very busy location facing the open square downtown. The house is simple in its layout and is utterly charming. The ghosts who inhabit the inn only add to the mystery.

KNOWN BUT TO GOD

On July 18, 1864, the Civil War struck the sleepy town of Stone Mountain, leaving death, destruction, and ghosts in its wake. On that day, General Kenner Garrard's Union cavalry moved from nearby Tucker, Georgia, into the area to destroy the tracks of the Georgia Railroad (one of five lines leading into nearby Atlanta), along with the water tank that serviced the locomotives. There was some opposition from the defending Confederate troops and regulars from Major General Joseph Wheeler's cavalry. The next day, the same units engaged in a minor battle again in the area, and the resulting carnage lead to many dead and wounded soldiers on each side. The adjoining town square was used as an open-air hospital, with the most severe surgical cases taken inside the inn.

General William Tecumseh Sherman's federal troops destroyed two miles of railroad track in the area—shaping the rails into the now-famous "Sherman neckties" by heating and then bending them around trees. The Stone Mountain community was at the end of the remaining usable portion of the railway, making this community both a site for a battle and a logical choice for a hospital. It was quite common for both Confederate and Union troops to take over several hotels or homes in villages near battles and turn them into hospitals.

While Union troops collected their dead for internment in northern states, Confederate soldiers—by this time clearly the losing side in this war—were often buried near their battle site. Also, with Confederates losing the war, there were generally more unknown Confederates than Union soldiers in the late battles of the war. Further, the war predated the ubiquitous "dog tags" which are used to identify contemporary battle dead; the human carnage was often quite severe and in some cases no identification was possible. Indeed, in hospitals of both sides, the injured who were strong enough to do so were sometimes known to carve their names on the walls at the head of their bed so that, if they died during the night, someone would at least know who they were. All his bespeaks the possibility of many disquieted spirits—spirits seeking some recognition of their life and their death.

The cemetery is only a few blocks from the Village Inn, and eight mass graves of Confederate dead are located there. Perhaps the historic marker in the cemetery says it best.

> Here sleep, known but to God, approximately one hundred and fifty Confederate soldiers, most of whom died from disease or wounds in the Confederate hospitals that were located near this spot. Some were killed in a skirmish with federal raiders near here on July 19, 1864. Although federal troops raided and burned part of this city, Confederate hospitals were not molested. Brave and gallant Confederate women rendered valuable aid in caring for soldiers in Confederate hospitals here and elsewhere.

Hundreds of men, in both blue and gray, must have died here. One can easily imagine the spirits of some of these men who died in the inn, whose remains lie unidentified three blocks away, wanting someone to acknowledge their life and death.

THE ANTICS OF FRANK NASH

Christi Collins, owner and manager of the inn today, tells of many strange happenings in the building. Perhaps one of the strangest of the manifestations involved a spirit that Collins has named Sergeant Frank Nash. When the inn was renovated in 1995, the owners at that time found soldiers' names carved into the walls on the second floor. Collins believes that some of these names might have been carved into the wall by soldiers who worried that they would die unidentified during the night. One of the boards held the name of Sergeant Frank Nash—presumably a Confederate soldier who died in the house, perhaps one of the unknowns now buried in the mass graves down the street.

The former owners reported that they kept board from the wall as an example of what they found during the renovation, but that they chose to cover over many other names during the work. It is interesting to note that, according to Clair Mohr-Drake, leader of the Georgia Haunt Hunt Team, renovation projects tend to bring out ghosts; perhaps that is the case here.

In 1995, those owners were not interested in either history or ghosts, and no inventory, photographs, or tracings were kept of the names that were covered in that renovation—only the one board with

There are mass graves in the Stone Mountain Cemetery, only four blocks from the haunted Village Inn. While soldiers' bodies lie here, their spirits seem to prefer the hospital where they died.

Nash's name carved into it was saved. However, the owners soon noted that, if they placed the board by the fireplace in the downstairs room in the evening, by morning it had been moved. One may well imagine that it was quite a conversation piece for visitors to the bed and breakfast, and no doubt the owners of any inn would share this interesting trivia about the house with their guests. Those owners ignored the phenomena when guests were present, since one of the guests could easily have moved the board during the evening. However, these owners soon noted the same manifestation occurred even when no guests were in the house! Sergeant Nash was, apparently, letting his presence be felt.

THE DESERTED BALLROOM

Reverend Jacob Stillwell purchased the inn at Stone Mountain in 1868, and made a home there with his wife and nine children. The inn was the only building in town that would hold such a large family. Of course, this Baptist minister of yesteryear did not believe in dancing, so he firmly announced that the ballroom which occupied the entire third floor would serve as a nursery and playroom for the children. Soon, Reverend Stillwell and his wife left on a trip, and as soon as his carriage was out of sight, tradition holds, his two oldest daughters sent out invitations to a dance, hired a small orchestra from Atlanta, and made good use of the ballroom. Of course, with Stone Mountain being a small village then, as indeed it is today, the reverend quickly heard of the soiré upon his return. He was so furious that he cut out the stairs to the third floor, thus sealing it off the entirely. In fact, Collins reports that until the renovation in 1995, there was no open stairway at all to this deserted ballroom.

The reverend passed away only a decade or so after purchasing the house but it remained in the Stillwell family for the next hundred years; for most of the 1900s, the inn was used as a boarding house. According to Collins, a large number of families in the Stone Mountain area still report some connection with the house. She is often told "My grandparents lived there for a time" or "I spent a year of my childhood here." Yet one can easily imagine an angry clergyman of yesteryear, vengeful in spirit, still supervising the home of his beloved daughters and their descendants, making certain that no dancing is taking place.

OTHER MANIFESTATIONS

Many guests have reported strange occurrences in the inn over the years and the place often attracts mediums (persons who believe they can "connect" with the spirits) as guests. Once two sisters visited the inn, and after Collins showed them around, one of the sisters—who had remained quiet during the tour—remained to speak to her.

"I don't know if you believe in this sort of thing, or even if you are open to this, but I am very sensitive to things of a paranormal nature, and I want to tell you that you have at least three spirits in this home," the woman explained. "I can feel them around you, but I feel like they are here to help you and protect you; not to harm you."

Collins thought at the time that the woman was "off her rocker." Still, it wasn't long before manifestations became apparent, and Collins herself became convinced that the inn was haunted. For example, Collins would note that things would move—apparently entirely by themselves. She has seen ink pens move across a desk, or a piece of foil slide across the kitchen counter. She also has a number of photographs that include unexplained "white lights" and other ghostly images.

After Collins and her husband purchased the house, they retained a house-keeper who had worked on the property for the previous several years. As the housekeeper got to know Collins, she began to open up with her fears about working in the house. In fact, the housekeeper reported to her new employer that one of the ghosts followed her up and down the stairs. The housekeeper soon found other employment; she was simply terrified of working in the old inn.

One of the most interesting aspects of this true haunting is the fact that Collins reported herself to be "something of a skeptic" of things supernatural. This lends some credibility to the story; however, this may be offset by the fact that having a friendly "ghost" around can only add some charm to a bed and breakfast business. Still, as well as the owners, others have reported these same phenomena.

SPIRITS UNKNOWN

The manifestations at the Stone Mountain Inn constitute a convincing haunting for a number of reasons. First, a wide number of different people have experienced something in the house and reported the same strange phenom-enon. Next, the sad history of the house and its environs suggest that they would be a rich background for ghosts. Unfortunately, there is little one can do to bring on a manifestation of these specters. As Collins says, "When you want it to happen, it doesn't." Consequently, should one choose to visit this wonderful old inn, rich in history, one should do so for the charm of the inn and the sur-rounding village because the ghosts may or may not show up.

Still, the spirits are there. Other than Sergeant Frank Nash, no identity for the ghostly apparitions have been suggested. One can only wonder if all of these manifestations would be—or could be—created by only one spirit. Alter-natively, do the ghosts of uncounted and unnamed soldiers who died long ago still demand to be noticed? This is the most pressing question of all—who are the unregistered guests at this quaint old inn? Please forgive me if I suggest the possibility of one hundred and fifty unknown answers, now resting in the local cemetery.

AN ARRAY OF ATLANTA SPECTERS

One may only assume that spirits are drawn to the objects and locations that they loved in life; most ghost tales and stories of true hauntings seem to support this notion. In fact, that is also why so many of us, the living, have been drawn to the Atlanta area. We shouldn't be surprised if an interesting array of specters share our passion for this beautiful city. I was not surprised that, with a bit of investigative work, so many spirits were uncovered here. I *was* surprised by the variety of these specters. Some of the resident ghosts appear to be

Modern Atlanta, while the cultural and financial capital of the New South, still hosts an array of ghosts, specters, and spiritual manifestations.

"chained spirits," condemned in the old DeKalb County Courthouse unjustly to death. One of the ghosts first reported here murdered a pet. Another is an imported ghost that arrived in Atlanta in 2002 on a piece of ornate woodwork. Spiritual variety seems to be the key.

Some ghosts are associated with commonly known places—Oglethorpe University, the DeKalb County Courthouse, and Oakland Cemetery. Still, many of the specters showed up in unexpected places—many in some of the fine old homes in Atlanta. Each of the specters described here has manifested itself before a number of people in a variety of ways, making these some of the most documented spirits in Atlanta. In many cases, there were a number of reliable witnesses available for interview. In each case, I have presented as much information as I could obtain, and the source from which the information came. While some of these spirits have been reported on before, the vast majority have not.

A DEADLY GHOST IN ANSLEY PARK

T om Harding was scared enough to break his lease and leave his apartment; he'd seen the ghostly outline of a young boy in his apartment one afternoon and it terrified him.

Harding is an engineer—a practical, down-to-earth man in his forties, married with two daughters. His professional education has equipped him with a strong science background. While Harding never believed in ghosts prior to living in the shared apartment off Montgomery Ferry in the Ansley Park area of Atlanta, his horrifying experiences in those quarters made him a confirmed believer. As he puts it, he is now a "big metaphysical fan."

During the 1970s, Harding lived for a brief time with two roommates and a ghost in this house just off Montgomery Ferry. The house itself is most undistinguished. It sits on Montgomery Ferry, probably built in the 1930s, and while one of the smaller homes in the neighborhood, its style fits with the other homes on its street. Made of brick and wood siding, the home has been

This 1930s house is divided into several apartments, and the main and basement floors include a resident ghost—perhaps a deadly one.

painted a soft color now, and the lawn is well landscaped. Back then, the house had been divided into three apartments: a basement apartment, a main-floor apartment, and an attic apartment. Harding and his roommates—his *mortal* roommates anyway—lived on the main floor. In the basement, the building had a common storage area, with lockable doors that opened into both the main-floor apartment through Harding's kitchen and into the basement apartment. Those two floors seemed to be the center of activity for this particular ghost.

In the Ansley Park apartment, keys would be moved overnight. Items left on the counter would not be there the next morning and they would later be located in strange places—under tables or chairs or in other rooms. Pictures were often overturned and items on the coffee table were moved and left in disarray; grocery bags were torn and emptied.

More chillingly, this specter also liked fire. On various evenings, candles were found spontaneously alight, and in one case, a fire was built in the fireplace with the damper closed. While some of these early manifestations were benign, it soon became apparent that this spirit could be not only dangerous, but deadly. Although Harding and one of his roommates smoked cigarettes, the other roommate did not, and yet, one evening, in the room of the non-smoker, the bedsheets suddenly caught aflame. The three roommates rushed into the bedroom only to find that the linens were burned in a two-feet circle, and a box of burned matches was located dead center in the ash.

GHOSTLY FEEDINGS

One of the first spiritual manifestations involved a ghostly feeding. Harding knew that his downstairs neighbor didn't care for him and his roommates a bit. They were young guys, in their mid-twenties, while she was an older woman, perhaps in her fifties, who lived alone. Because the guys had always been polite to the older woman, they never understood the animosity she apparently felt for them. With a belligerent ghost living in the mix, only trouble could result.

One evening Harding and one of his roommates were awakened in the middle of the night by the Atlanta police, who asked if they had entered the basement apartment. Apparently the old woman, after working the night-shift at an Ansley Park drugstore, had reported that someone had entered her apartment, gone into the refrigerator, opened some milk and spilled it all over the counter. Of course Harding and his roommates had not entered the apartment—they could gain access only to the shared basement storage area, not the apartment in the basement. For them to enter her apartment, either the woman would have to unlock her access door or the guys would have to break in the door into her apartment. Of course, the police asked to see the storage area, and noted that the access door was locked on both sides: on the side of the guys' apartment and on the side of the basement apartment itself. It was apparent that the police had awakened the guys from a sound sleep earlier and the officers quickly became convinced of the guys innocence.

After the officers were convinced that Harding and his roommates had indeed been asleep, they told the men that the renter in the basement had called the police and told them of the strange milk spill in her apartment. The old woman had reported this as a burglary, which led to the police call in the middle of the night. Of course, the police could not establish any evidence for a break-in, and this crime really involved nothing more than spilled milk. Had that been the only strange occurrence on Montgomery Ferry, this tale would have ended as merely an unexplained evening experienced by an older woman in a basement apartment. However, the same incident was repeated a number of times over the next few months.

In fact, after a couple of odd happenings the basement, Harding and his two roommates likewise noticed the same type of thing in their own home. Their refrigerator would be opened during the day when none of the guys were around, and food taken or spilled on the floor.

THE KILLING

O ne day, roommate Phillips purchased a little puppy. All of the roommates enjoyed having the dog around and he soon became a favorite pet. During the workday, the dog was left inside the apartment and would be walked when one or another of the guys came home.

One day, they found that the spirit had paid a visit again. Phillips entered the apartment and found that the bread—usually kept in the top cabinet above the refrigerator—had been taken down, opened, and scattered on the kitchen floor. There was no possibility that the small dog could have gotten on top of the refrigerator and gotten into the bread bag by himself—the refrigerator was simply too high for the dog to have gotten at it. Thinking merely that he had stumbled upon another ghostly visit, he began to clean it up. Then he realized that the dog was nowhere to be seen and began to call out for him. He quickly covered each room in the apartment and soon found the animal dead. The dog had been suffocated with the bread bag over its head, and it had been suspended with his bagged head wedged in a tight curve in the lower drainpipe beneath the toilet. The door to the bathroom was shut and, of course, his small puppy didn't—*couldn't*—shut doors. With the its head in that position, the dog could not get his legs up to wrestle the bag from its head. With this horrifying instance, the spiritual manifestation became deadly.

THE IMAGE OF A GHOST

One day, while Harding was home alone, he finally saw the specter who have caused so much trouble. The sight—a manifestation of a young boy—was horrifying.

"I was sitting in the living room, listening to music, and I turned and looked into the dinning room," Harding explained. "In the corner of the dinning room, I saw a figure . . . this figure was an aura. It was invisible in the middle--as if you are standing in a window and bright light is coming in. You can see the light around [the figure], but you can't see me. You've got an outline, but the figure was invisible— it was a silver aura, kind of misty, and extended eight o twelve inches out from this figure. I was totally startled—totally scared, and I got up and walked towards it from the living room into the dinning room [through] a double-arch doorway."

"It was three feet out from the corner. It was a profile--I could see the ears, the legs, the arms—perhaps twenty to twenty-two feet from me. I got to within about five feet, and walked around it and caught a profile of it," Harding continued. "As I walked around it, it continued to look into the living room. And as I walked around it, I could see its forehead, its nose, its mouth, and its chin from a side angle. I was freaked; I was totally freaked, then it turned and looked at me.

"It scared me totally out of my wits. I went out of the house; I locked the back door, and I walked up the street to a payphone and started calling someone to come get me. I was scared to death. I can't remember ever spending even twenty-four hours in that house after that."

Understandably, Harding and his roommates asked to break their lease, and they moved from the house shortly after that experience.

To this day neither Harding nor his roommate Phillips have any idea who this ghost might be. Harding and Phillips have not remained in contact during the intervening twenty-five or so years since they shared quarters in Ansley Park; they had not seen each other in at least five years. In fact, Harding did not even contact his old roommate prior to my interview of Harding. As Harding explained it, he wanted a "double blind" confirmation of his own memory of these experiences and gave me contact information for Phillips only after he and I had talked. In an interview with Phillips, it soon became apparent that he wasn't quite sure how to take my inquiry about these ghostly manifestations from his youth.

Therefore, after my interview with Harding, I called Phillips "cold." (Imagine a call coming in unexpectedly about a ghost sighting twenty-five years previous!). During that initial interview, I didn't tell Phillips which of his old roommates I had talked with previously, and he couldn't guess which roommate it might have been. This adds credence to my assessment of Harding's overall stability and trustworthiness. Phillips confirmed the experiences of strange misplacement of objects in the apartment and of the bizarre suffocation of the puppy, as reported originally by Harding. The third roommate from those years could not be located, and Harding reports that he never believed that these were ghostly experiences at any rate.

Long after this experience—in the mid-1990s—Harding drove by the old house in Ansley Park and saw his former landlords working in the yard. He asked about other experiences, and they reported that there had been no recent experiences of any ghostly manifestations at all.

Still, Harding is firm in his assessment—with the assurance that only a man of science can show. "I know what I saw," he insists, "and it scared me to death!"

Although he had never had such an experience before living in the Montgomery Ferry apartment, Harding reports that has since seen several ghosts in the older home in which he now lives. His wife and daughters have not experienced such sightings. These experiences have made Harding a believer in what he refers to as "group consciousness."

A GHOST IN MIDTOWN

G hosts may make their domiciles in many places, but finding one in an apartment can be quite daunting. This apartment house on Eleventh Street, near Piedmont Park, was originally a single-family home; it likely was built between the turn of the last century and the 1920s. Although the area was located outside the Confederate defensive line that ran across Peachtree Street approximately where Third Street now crosses Peachtree, nothing of consequence occurred here during the Civil War—the area was not settled then and was too close to Atlanta to be involved in the Battle of Peachtree Creek.

Rather this area of houses and apartments was a later addition to the city, springing up in the last decades of the nineteenth century. By the early 1990s, the house on Eleventh Street was divided up into several apartments. Elizabeth Korach moved into the building in 1994. Korach didn't realize at the time that a ghost—apparently a "protective" ghost who is also something of a prankster— also lived in the home!

In this older house in Midtown, only a few yards from sunny Piedmont Park, an unquiet spirit roams.

Renovation work was being done on Korach's building at the time of her move-in. According to specialists in hauntings, renovations to older buildings can bring out ghostly activity. Apparently the spirits don't abide change and continue to wander in the familiar pathways in the home (which is one reason why ghosts apparently "travel through walls" when, for example, walls are constructed where doors once were).

GHOSTLY MANIFESTATIONS

Because of the ongoing renovation work, Korach initially stored many of her belongings in a laundry room at the rear of the house. Her bedroom was toward the back of the house and the furniture was arranged so that the foot of the bed faced the wall which she shared with the utility room. On her first night in the new apartment, just as she lay down to sleep, a box of her belongings fell off a shelf in the laundry room. As Korach later reported, "I didn't think too much of it at the time. I just assumed that I had positioned a stack of the boxes poorly, and they toppled."

However, the next day, she restacked the boxes, carefully assuring that they were absolutely stable. Again, just as she got into bed, one of the boxes fell. According to Korach, this same phenomenon was repeated for four consecutive nights, and each time Korach was quite sure she had stacked the boxes in a stable manner. While this seemed quite weird, Korach chose to view these occurrences as an interesting result of living in an older house. In fact, Korach reports having felt no apprehension at all.

"The fact is that I was absolutely unafraid and actually felt kind of comforted and happy about it," she says. "The presence there seemed to provide pleasant company for me. I was comfortable with the situation."

In the following couple of months, Korach noticed additional strange manifestations. Suddenly, a cabinet door would open by itself, coming to rest about a foot or two from the doorframe and then stopping just as abruptly. One evening, as Korach was seated on her couch reading, there was suddenly a loud knocking at the window directly opposite her seat. It was still daylight outside, and Korach reports that she had "a very clear view of the window which was not more than fifteen feet away." When she looked up, there was no one there.

On another evening, Korach was again on the couch reading and suddenly felt an odd warmth on her feet. When she looked up she saw that her cat was on the floor staring wide-eyed at an area on the floor next to her.

"The warmth on my feet was intermittent and somewhat damp," she explains. "It was actually as if someone were sitting on the floor next to me, leaning on the couch and breathing on my feet. I know that this is very strange and it gives me the creeps to think of it now."

In spite of this creepy feeling on that occasion, Korach reports that overall she did not feel fear during most of these encounters. Instead, she reports a sense of well-being.

KORACH'S FIRST SIGHTING

After a number of haunting experiences, Korach finally began to catch glimpses of this ghost.

"There were, here and there, a couple of instances, too, where I would catch a glimpse of someone, and then they would shift and disappear," Korach explains. "It was usually just a portion of the body--typically the upper torso. I would get a flash of a shoulder or the back of a head. It was always the same "person" and seemed like a guy who had reddish blond hair with maybe a beard. He wore a white shirt—maybe a T-shirt. He was probably in his mid- to late-thirties."

THE NEW ROOMMATE

When a new roommate—a very mortal roommate—Julie Morton moved in, Korach told her of the "ghost in the house." Morton was unconvinced. She reports that she was not particularly concerned with either the ghost or with her long-time friend reporting this strange phenomena. Morton had known Korach since their high-school days in Missouri, and while she did find this ghostly tale to be a curious thing, she wanted to live with her longtime friend. In fact, at that time, Morton considered herself something of a cynic concerning these ghostly phenomenon, and over time she forgot Korach's caution concerning their resident ghost. This changed rather quickly one evening at 4:01 A. M.

Morton awoke one September evening in 1995 because she sensed that someone was watching her; she awoke to find a male in the corridor between her bedroom and the bathroom. He had light brown or dark blond hair and was in his early thirties. He was wearing a sleeveless T-shirt. He was not transparent in any sense and Morton reports that she saw him quite clearly. He was somewhat backlit from the streetlights coming through the bathroom windows. She was not unduly disturbed, since she immediately sensed a caring, brotherly concern from the apparition. She glanced quickly at the digital clock on her bedside table, noting the time—4:01 A. M.

"When he looked at me," Korach explains, "he looked at me in almost a caring, big brotherly sort of way, as if he would have watched a little sister sleep--just happened to walk by and paused to look. When I said hey to him and kind of sat up, he turned towards me as if he heard me, and was surprised--maybe kind of taken aback a bit that I had seen him. . . .

"He was about five feet away, basically at the foot of my bed, and he was turning as if to walk by the head of my bed which would have led out into the living room. But as he turned he dissipated and I couldn't see him anymore."

The entire episode took only two or three seconds, and Morton reports that she was quite "freaked out," but she didn't feel any intense threat or any need to leave the room because she didn't feel threatened at all. Again, Morton did not believe in ghosts at the time. She had never previously seen one herself, and she didn't feel fear at that moment.

Morton didn't immediately tell her roommate. Rather, she calmly contemplated the experience for a few minutes, asking what the experience might have been. She remembers noting the time again at 4:15 A. M.

"I would like to point out that I sat up contemplating this for about fifteen or twenty minutes, watching the time pass, so I know I was awake."

There is no hysterical behavior here, and Morton didn't immediately try to validate her experience by telling others or asking questions. This lends some credibility to her account.

In fact, when the two roommates spoke the next day, she didn't initially talk about this as a ghostly experience, but rather tried to explain it to herself in some fashion. Morton questioned Korach about the possibility that Korach had brought a friend home after her late-night shift ended.

Korach recalls Morton's questioning that morning: "I was working as a waitress at a bar just a couple of blocks away and often went out after my shift with coworkers. I would usually come by the apartment to change before going out and sometimes brought home a friend to walk to the next destination with, who would wait for me as I changed. I'm sure that Julie had to often deal with the guests passing through her space to get to the bathroom on such occasions; she seemed ready to accept her ghost sighting just as that. Apparently she mistook the ghost for one of my friends at first and started to say hi. The next day she asked me about what I did the night before and who it was that I brought over. I said that I stayed at a friend's that night and hadn't come home after work at all."

After this discussion, Morton and Korach compared their experiences with the apparition, with each questioning the other about what they had seen and experienced. The apparition Morton had seen was a white male, approximately thirty to forty years old, who was wearing a white T-shirt. His hair, she described, was dirty blond.

When I interviewed both Korach and Morton, I was struck as they had been by the similarity of their sightings of this apparition. Both gave similar accounts of the apparation's gender, race, age, dress, and hair color. This spirit is quite consistent in his appearance to two different witnesses, each of whom was initially somewhat cynical on the subject of ghosts overall, and neither of whom had had such experiences before. In short, this is quite a believable manifestation.

OTHERS EXPERIENCE THE MIDTOWN GHOST

Korach reports that some of her friends and guests thought they had seen or heard strange things in the house on Eleventh Street. On one occasion, a male guest jumped up and went into the laundry room, the same room where Korach's boxes had fallen earlier. When Korach asked why, he said he thought he saw someone in the room.

The next occupants of this apartment—a couple—reported experiences with this apparition after Korach and Morton moved out. The scenes which the new occupants (casual acquaintances of Morton's and Korach's) reported to them were much more violent and threatening, involving horrific scenes with "bloody children's bodies near a baby carriage." Those occupants moved out within two months, because of these violent images.

It is interesting to note that these latter experiences were quite threatening, compared to the generally kindly feelings experienced by Morton and Korach, and that begs the question, why does this apparition manifest himself so differently?

"I find it very interesting that Julie and I would have such very different experiences from [those of the next occupant] and her friend," says Korach. "Perhaps this ghost is gender biased and didn't like the new male presence? Maybe Julie and I are just so likeable that an otherwise hellish haunting would be nice to us? Just some extra things to wonder about after my experiences [on Eleventh Street]."

A GHOST UNKNOWN

Each of these young women is moving forward with their lives; each has subsequently married, and Korach has moved out of town. Morton's husband is considering a career in the ministry and Morton realizes how such a career may impact her life. Neither Morton nor Korach reported any experiences with ghostly apparitions either before or since their experiences in this home. In fact, both are somewhat reluctant to discuss this matter; Morton, in particular, noted that she felt almost "apologetic" for having had this experience. While this seems to lend some credibility to their experiences with this ghost in Midtown, there is not much to base research on for this particular spirit.

Morton once noted in our discussions that she felt this ghost to be from the 1930s or 1940s. Other than that impression neither has any sense of who this ghost may be.

Sometimes, as in this story, ghostly apparitions can not be explained by research into local history or research on the immediate haunted environment. We are left with only questions. Who may this restless spirit be? Moreover, how can we assist this man to find his peace?

THE SMOKY GHOST OF TUCKER

The smell—the smell of burned wood, insulation, and smoke—was there with her, right there in the car, and it shocked her. Teresa Lass was driving home from a meeting of the board of a major Atlanta museum. This was only a week and a half after she had buried her fiancé Max. She still hadn't gotten used to his absence and dreaded having to chair the meeting on that spring evening, but there was no one else to do that duty, and even after the death of a loved one, life does goes on.

Driving home after the meeting, Lass reflected on the way he always asked that she phone him when she left the museum area late at night. He'd always been concerned for her safety, and she soon realized that on this evening, no one would be calling; she began to cry, as his recent death was re-experienced, yet again. As the sadness swept over her, she reached the stoplight on the corner of Brockett Road and Lawrenceville Highway in Tucker, and there she first noticed it–the smoky burned smell. Chill bumps covered her arms; she knew she was smelling the last smell he would have known—the smell of burning wood, sideboard, and insulation, (but thankfully not flesh). He had died only ten days before, trying to escape a fire in the home they were redoing together. His body had not burned, instead he'd died, as so many do, from the deadly, all-engulfing fumes, from smoke inhalation.

Now his spirit was in the car with her. Even in her shock she knew to scan the gauges on her dashboard—engine heat, oil pressure—and saw nothing was amiss with the engine. Even before she looked at the instruments, she was certain she would find no car problems. She knew it was him.

Finally, she asked, "Max, is that you?" She was partially hoping to hear an answer; partially hoping to hear nothing.

"I knew it was Max. I said, 'Max, is it you?' I didn't expect an answer, but just to acknowledge his presence in that car with me. It was strangely comforting," Lass explains, "and stayed for a full two or three minutes, and then it departed as quickly as it came."

Humans have such capacity for mixed emotions, it's interesting how one can feel frightened and comforted at the same time. How would anyone feel when they believed they had confronted the ghost of a recently deceased loved one? Lass believed, and still believes, that Max was checking on her well-being, and perhaps saying goodbye.

A TERRIBLE DEATH, A BENEVOLENT SPIRIT

I had met Lass socially and when the topic of my book came up in conversation, she began to discretely inquire as to my beliefs. I had the sense that she wanted to say more, and after finding that I intended to approach each Atlanta haunting with respect, she shared this story with me. The next weekend, I visited the house in Tucker, just a few minutes east of Interstate 285, and Lass showed me where Max had died.

"Right there, in the corner of this bedroom by the door into the hallway, is where the firemen found his body," Lass explained. "He'd gotten out of the bed that was in the corner of the room by the window. He made it about six feet across the floor before he passed out. The fireman said that if he'd made it another four feet, he'd have made it out of the house alive. He would have been only partially conscious, and he couldn't make it."

The fire started in the back fireplace, approximately forty feet from where Max was sleeping. The wood must have sparked up after Max went to bed; he had probably gone to bed thinking the fire was out. A log shifted and tipped out of the fireplace onto the floor—a rare event, but too common in the eyes of firefighters. One hates to think of the terrible consequences.

A death by house fire is often a death of suffocation, and sometimes of horrible terror and pain. I hesitate to state this so blatantly here, but it does warrant pointing out that even with the terror Max must have felt in his last mortal moments, he is not a malevolent spirit. Even after this terrible death, he has not returned to frighten, but rather to comfort.

After the deadly fire on that spring evening of 2001, Lass was left with the shell of the house she and Max had been refurbishing. It was a family home and her mother lived next door. She decided to fix the house up anyway and move in, and I saw the house while it was under construction for the second time. It was an eerie feeling, having her show me the location of his body. I felt an intimacy with this ghost that I rarely felt with the others as I wrote this book. Here a man had lived and died, and I was being told this spirit's tale by someone only one year distant from the actual events. I could feel Lass's pain still, but she wanted this story told, a story of love after death.

THE SPIRIT TRAVELS ON A CLOUD OF SMOKE

Several days after Lass had her ghostly experience, she talked with Max's mother and learned of a similar experience. One April 2001 evening, about a year after Max died, his mother's home in a small town in Arkansas filled up with a smoky smell. Both she and her husband noted the smell. It was so intense that they both got up and looked all over the house checking for fire, only to find that nothing was amiss. As it turns out, these were not Max's only manifestations.

Two days after Max appeared in the car with Lass, his sister's house in upstate New York also filled up with a smoky smell. At that point, Max had manifested his presence in the homes of the three people who he loved most. The sister believed, as did Lass, that Max was checking in and saying goodbye.

This evidence is telling simply because several independent witnesses, separated geographically, noted the same phenomena. Of course, witnesses can often convince each other of a phenomena, but Lass is quite down to earth, a teacher in the public schools in metro Atlanta. She assured me that her prospective in-laws were quite normal and not "hysterical" people in any sense.

Unfortunately, Max's parents have since passed away, and Lass, who never got to know her potential sister in-law very well, is no longer certain of her whereabouts. Thus, only Lass could be interviewed for this story.

THE FIANCÉ COMES CALLING STILL, FROM TIME TO TIME

Lass reports that Max visited for a time after these initial manifestations. While she has never seen a spirit or any type of visual manifestation, she reports that she would often smell the burned smoke smell at special occasions in her life, both in the house and elsewhere. It was as if Max wanted to have his presence known to her at important moments in her life. She also relates the story of the lights outside her house.

The lights were motion-sensitive outdoor lights that had been installed incorrectly. In fact, prior to Max's death, the lights did not sense movement in the yard, and thus turn on, as they were supposed to do. In fact, one would have to actually walk up to the lights and touch them for them to come on. However, after Max died, those lights started popping on all the time. Lass reports that while still inside the house, one can now step up to the backdoor and the lights will come on. Max seems to be protecting Lass.

That is where we shall leave this specter. While many experience hauntings as scary, Lass feels a sense of closure here, as does the rest of Max's family. Even in the instance of a horrible death by fire, this spirit has found a way to manifest itself with a sense of love and helpful caring. Perhaps that is the lesson to be drawn from this spirit—that even in adversity, we will all ultimately be remembered for our loving, caring deeds for our fellow man. Thus, let us wish Max well on his unending journey and thank his spirit respectfully for this thoughtful lesson of love.

A HAUNTING IN KIRKWOOD

MR. RUGGLES COMES HOME

It was Christmas break in 1989 and John was the first living person to see the spirit. He was visiting his mother over the holidays and entered the house with a school friend through a door on the south side of the house. Glancing down a dim hallway, approximately twelve feet away, he saw a man standing there. His first thought was that a burglar had broken into the house; he reached for the light switch in the darkened hallway, and when the light came on the man simply disappeared. Of course, this shocked both John and his friend—both had seen the man quite clearly, and neither had seen him move in any direction or try to make any type of escape—he had simply vanished.

The house's main-floor central hallway opens into the back of the living room, and other doors open from the hall into the dining room, a bathroom, and a bedroom. An intruder would have had plenty of doors to exit through. Still, neither John nor his friend saw the man make a motion. At that point, neither John nor his friend wished to stay in the house and they left hurriedly, as one may imagine. John called his mother immediately after this frightening occurrence, and when the family investigated later, no reason for this spectral apparition was found and no windows or doors were broken or ajar.

While that was the first, and one of the eeriest experiences with this ghost in Kirkwood, it certainly was not the last. In fact, some suspect that the spirit of original builder of the house, Frank A. Ruggles, come home from time to time.

THE HISTORY OF THE HOUSE

L ike many places in southeast Atlanta, this house, just north of Interstate 20 on Howard Street, sits near battle lines from the Battle of Atlanta. For that reason, one might well expect many spirits here; however, all indications concerning the spirit at Howard Street indicated that these spirits stem from a later point in Atlanta's history, the turn of the last century to be precise.

The Kirkwood section of Atlanta is filled with many fine homes dating from

This distinctive turn-of-the-twentieth-century home in the Kirkwood neighborhood is still haunted by its builder—and perhaps a the spirit of a little girl as well.

1900 through 1920, and a number of them were built by Ruggles. He was a bold designer and builder, and his houses featured may unusual features such as vast porches, deeply stained paneling made of a variety of woods, decorative fountains on the grounds, floor plans that were much more complex than the traditional central hallway with side rooms, and exquisite woodwork around doors and windows. In 1909, Ruggles decided to build a home for his wife Katherine, their children Clarence and Olive, and himself. He chose this area of the growing town of Atlanta. Like many older communities, Kirkwood had originally grown as a separate small "crossroads" type of town, only to be overgrown by the ever-enlarging city of Atlanta. In fact, many long-time residents of Kirkwood still talk of "downtown," meaning not downtown Atlanta a few miles distance, but rather the small cluster of stores in the heart of old Kirkwood. Ruggles wisely purchased a ten-acre track of land in what was to become a very nice subdivision and chose to build his house on the property's most prominent point, a small hill on the southwest corner of his land.

On his own home Ruggles spared no expense. The design is unique, and it is preserved in much its original state by current occupants, Wayne Carey and Kay Coffman.

Carey, who is interested in both local history and period homes, has traced the house's history and knows all of the owners dating from the home's completion in the summer of 1910. Frank died in 1938, and the house went to Katherine who passed away in 1942. The home was then inherited by their daughter Olive and her husband, with brother Clarence living in an outbuilding on the property at various times. The home stayed in the Ruggles family until the 1960s. Carey, who has been quite interested in these manifestations, indicated there were no extant pictures of the Ruggleses. In fact, some of the neighbors recall that Katherine destroyed all of the family photographs for some unknown reason—an interesting fact, in a day when photos of family were both much more rare than they are today, and were also much more treasured.

The fact that the house remained in the hands of a single family for two generations probably accounts for the fact that this home is such a well-preserved example of architecture from early Arts and Crafts style. Still, at various points the home was divided up into smaller apartments, with some modifications made to the back of the house in particular.

Carey and Coffman have, for the most part, restored the home to its original layout, and have filled it with wonderful vintage and antique objects that beautifully preserve the flavor of early-twentieth-century life.

A HEAVY BREATHER

Carey and Coffman are two delightful people, each of whom was most interested in sharing their story of haunting. Each has had some unusual experiences in this old house. For example, when Carey and Coffman first moved into the house, they were using an upstairs bedroom and bath. Carey was in the upstairs bathroom and heard fitful breathing, then snoring, coming from the bedroom. He knew that Coffman and the dogs were in the bedroom. He thought, "My God, she's got a sinus problem!"

"I said, 'Are you asleep?' And nothing," Carey continues, "so I finished doing what I was doing, and I went in and noticed that she was still awake, so I said, 'There was this incredible snoring, heavy breathing, labored breathing coming from here.'

"Kay responded that, 'It wasn't us!' But the interesting thing was that Fowler [one of their dogs] heard it. At that point, Fowler got up off the bed and went looking around the room, sniffing towards the bathroom."

Neither Carey nor Coffman ever figured out what Fowler was responding to, unless he, like Carey, also had heard the labored breathing.

THE SPIRIT OF A LOST CHILD

Other strange things have happened to both Carey and Coffman in this haunted house. Once, Coffman was on the landing about half way up to the second floor when she experienced an uneasy feeling.

"I was going upstairs; the upstairs has always been a little . . . just doesn't feel quite right sometimes. It's like there is somebody there, and you don't ever see them or anything, but you turn around because you think they are behind you. You sort of *feel* them.

"One day, when I was on my way up there, there was a voice that said, 'Mama, Mama,' over and over. When I got up there, I thought, 'Oh my God!' We didn't have any cats or animals up there then and it sounded like a little girl; it was a little girl's voice, just like she was calling for her mother."

Olive Ruggles spent most of her childhood in the house and, upon inheriting the house when her mother died, continued to live there with her husband until her death in the 1960s. A spirit with that much history in one home could very easily become attached to that location. Also, this feminine manifestation suggests the possibility that there are several spirits in the house. One would assume that the spirit of the man in the hallway would not subsequently manifest as a small girl.

DOES CLARENCE YET VISIT THE SCENE OF HIS MURDER?

Still this doesn't exhaust the bizarre and unusual manifestations of the Ruggles house; in fact, we have no clear evidence of who the male spirit in the hallway is! For example, there is a local legend—told to the current owners by a neighbor a decade ago, suggesting that Clarence Ruggles, Frank's son, was murdered on the property in the early 1960s. Prior to building the house on the property, the elder Ruggles had built a small workshop that now stands behind the main house. Ruggles used the shop to do his cabinetwork and woodwork for the other houses he was building all over Atlanta. In the early 1960s Olive and her husband were living in the house itself, and because she and her brother were not getting along at that point, Clarence was living in the workshop. In fact, their relationship was so strained during the 1940s that Olive would not even allow Clarence to draw water from the well on the property; he had to take water from the neighbor who subsequently shared this story with Carey and Coffman.

Apparently, Clarence was quite an eccentric character. He used to wear white Panama suits in a time when most men wore nothing but dark-colored suits with white shirts. He also loved animals and lived with at least six dogs of all types. He was observed to walk through a back alley to the restaurants in the downtown area of Kirkwood—only two blocks away—to scrounge for food. He had a reputation for being quite cheap, and he searched for scraps that were about to be tossed out, saying the food was for his dogs. The suspicion was that he ate some of the food too.

Although he had a reputation for thrift, Clarence was also known to have some money. He loaned money to others to purchase homes in the area—in those days many private citizens offered funds for home mortgages—and he speculated on some property in Atlanta as well.

Clarence was found dead in his bed in the woodshop behind the house one morning, bled to death. Either he was mugged in the alley the evening before as he walked home and thought he could tend his own wounds, or he had been robbed and killed in his own bed—the case is still unsolved.

Perhaps this spirit in the hallway, and the "bathroom breather" is the spirit of a man raised in an impressive house but who was not even permitted to visit there later in life.

THE MANIFESTATIONS CONTINUE

In the early months of 2000, Carey had a ghostly encounter while he was in the downstairs bathroom. By that time, Carey and Coffman's pets had aged somewhat and had difficulty in going up the stairs at night. As a result, Coffman and Carey had moved their bedroom to one of the downstairs rooms and Carey was using the bathroom that opened into the central hallway. He distinctly heard the door separating the living room from the central hallway close shut. This door was within ten feet of the location where their visiting son had seen the spirit of the man in the darkened hallway years before, but on this occasion, no apparition was seen. In fact, unlike their son, neither Carey nor Coffman has ever seen a spirit in the house.

This manifestation—the sound of the door slamming shut—has been repeated several times over the years, and on one occasion the sound of a door slamming shut was accompanied by the sound of footsteps walking down the hallway.

"That time, I actually opened the bathroom door and looked out," Carey explained, "and there was nobody there, of course. I remember thinking, O. K., these events seem to be staggered—a year passes, with nothing, but then things happen."

Another manifestation took place once again in the downstairs bathroom, adjacent to the central hallway. Carey was taking a shower and noticed that the mirror seemed to "wipe itself" as if some invisible hand holding a towel had wiped the condensation off the face of the glass. Carey noted over the next few days, even though the mirror had long since dried up, it seemed to hold the wipe marks for a number of days.

The latest occurrence took place in the dining room off the downstairs hallway. Carey was reaching for a package that was in one of the dining room chairs one evening, and it seemed that someone or something pulled the package away from him. His immediate thought was that the spirits were here again.

THE INVESTIGATION

The spiritual manifestations are typically centered around the downstairs hallway, and this is where John had seen the spirit. On the other hand, Coffman's experience of the spiritual voice of the young girl took place in the upstairs rooms.

Both Carey and Coffman believe their house to be haunted, but neither is terribly afraid. Coffman reported that the first experience was really scary, but now these mortal owners merely notice with some interest the occasional ghostly manifestation. Their attitude seems to be that while each time the spirits visit, something unnerving occurs, the spirits merely wish to check up on their old house once in a while.

As one interested in verifying these phenomenon, it is always key to have a couple of witnesses for any manifestation, and these two homeowners were as reliable as any witness one is likely to encounter. It is apparent that they are quite sincere and are not troubled living with these spirits.

So, what are we to make of this manifestation? Are there multiple spirits residing in the Ruggles house? Perhaps a young female spirit resides upstairs, and one or more male spirits frequent the central hallway downstairs. It would seem that at least two, and perhaps three spirits, have some reason for visiting their mortal home, and while these ghosts seem to be relatively benign, spirits should never be ignored. First of all, these spirits apparently wish to be noticed. More importantly, we may anticipate that long after Carey and Coffman have moved on, these spirits will be around to check up on the future owners of their beloved old home in Kirkwood.

MESSAGES FROM THE DEAD
THE MILAM HOUSE GHOST OF COLLEGE PARK

Only a few days after the funeral, in the darkened bedroom in the house on Pierce Road, Frances Milam feels his spirit lightly tapping her shoulder. Her dead nephew wants to talk, to communicate with the living. When this unusual communication began, he had been dead for only a couple of days, but his spirit told her to pick up her pen and write, and she did.

This eerie "spirit writing" scene repeats itself frequently, over many years. During the first encounter, Milam wrote until she had something of the order of ten letters to various individuals—many to people she did not even know. These are the now-famous messages from the dead.

There are also other manifestations of this spirit. At times, Milam's son and his wife have heard things falling in rooms which were unoccupied in the house. At other times, various objects have been moved by unseen hands.

DR. MARBY, IN LIFE

This ghost is presumed to be Dr. Bob Mabry, the nephew of Frances Milam of the College Park area in Atlanta. Dr. Mabry was a specialist in emergency medicine with a family and a successful career in Florida. At the time of his death, his aunt thought his life was going well. She had become very close to Dr. Mabry—virtually a surrogate mother—when his real mother passed away during his childhood. To the outside observer, Dr. Mabry's life was nothing out of the ordinary—merely family man and a successful physician—but apparently he was haunted by private demons.

SPIRIT WRITING

Milam had studied spiritualism previously, and was familiar with the idea of "spirit writing," but this had never happened to her. Still, she typed the letters as dictated by Dr. Marby's spirit and sent them on to the various addressees in Florida. Many of the recipients were surprised, and somewhat skeptical, when they learned of how the letters came to be written, but as they read the letters, they found there was at least one hidden message, perhaps a reference to a shared incident or private joke that no one else would know about. Milam reports that these individuals had to believe at that point.

Milam sensed the presence of her nephew quite often. His spirit uses her hand to write the messages, often warning adolescents of the dangers of suicide. This spirit is not restless in the usual sense, and seems to be one Atlanta haunting that is beneficial, in the sense that his warnings against suicide has been shared with a number of different individuals.

Although the story has been reported by two previous ghostbusters—Arthur Myers and Dennis William Hauck--I can neither confirm nor deny it and the ghost of College Park must still be viewed as speculative Atlanta legend.

THE HAUNTED AUDITORIUM AT
OGLETHORPE UNIVERSITY

This spirit loves Oglethorpe University, as do many living students, alumni, and faculty at this historic seat of higher learning. Today's students at Oglethorpe have chosen a private liberal arts education and, by and large, they clearly love their learning experience on the beautiful campus on Peachtree Industrial Boulevard. Oglethorpe has a rich history of scholarship dating from 1835 and prides itself on offering a unique blend of liberal arts, with a focus on practical education for today's changing world. Sidney Lanier, Georgia's most famous poet of the nineteenth century was an Oglethorpe student in 1860, and many other distinguished alumni have made contributions to Georgia and the nation. The Georgia Shakespeare Festival—appropriately enough given the bard's interest in ghosts—has long been in residence there.

In spite of this rich history, Oglethorpe students--like students everywhere—will sometimes compare notes on this or that aspect of campus life and complain. One of the early manifestations in the haunted auditorium at Oglethorpe involved just such a student gripe session.

Troy Dwyer and several other students were working in the Lupton Auditorium in the fall of 1990. Of course, they were aware of rumors of a ghost in the old building, but none of the students were ever terribly uncomfortable working in the haunted auditorium. Further, majoring in theater at Oglethorpe required uncounted hours working in the auditorium that served as playhouse, set design and construction workshop, wardrobe department, and virtually every other type of space required in to produce theater.

One student, being somewhat theatrical in nature anyway, was complaining about various things at Oglethorpe—cafeteria cooking, classes, homework, etc.—until the complaints reached crescendo levels, and that is when it happened.

Dwyer saw the curtains on the south wall—curtains that had been pulled tightly shut so that no outsider could see the set in advance of the opening—fly up by themselves, one after another, in sequence all the way down the side wall. Then the curtains along the back wall were quickly raised by a ghostly hand, most of the way across the back wall towards the entrance. Not only were they moving by themselves, they were doing so in sequence! All told, seven separate curtains went up by themselves that day. Dwyer also remembers a "rumble" of some type; one of the other students present that day stated that she felt some vibration through the stage floor itself!

Clearly, this spirit doesn't like any loud complaints about his beloved university! What happened to the student with the complaints? She immediately apologized to Wendell, the spirit in this old auditorium. The complaints were heard no more.

THE NAMING OF THE GHOST

D r. Wendell Brown was regarded as an excellent professor, a real mentor to students, teaching in the humanities at Oglethorpe from the 1940s through the 1960s. Beloved by his students, he returned that admiration by giving students his time unceasingly—the mark of a truly great faculty member. While carrying a full load of classes, he also advised the drama club and directed a play each and every semester, year in and year out. (His wife Eve helped with sets and costumes.)

Dr. Wendell Brown was a beloved faculty member and still remains constant in his support for theater at Oglethorpe University, where his spirit is said to haunt Lupton Auditorium.

By all accounts, Dr. Brown went the extra mile. He loved theater, believing that drama, comedy, tragedy, and the arts in general bring an enjoyment to life, as well as a deeper understanding of the human condition. Moreover, he was able to communicate that insight and love for theater to generation after generation of his students. Perhaps his spirit still seeks to impart that same message in the old theater—it would be only one additional indicator of his dedication.

LUPTON HALL: A BUILDING MADE FOR A GHOST

Lupton Hall is one of the three original buildings constructed at Oglethorpe. The university, originally founded in 1835 in Midway, Georgia, was rechartered in Atlanta in 1913, having died for a period after the

This gothic style building looks as if it was *made for a ghost.*

Civil War. In 1920 the beautiful gothic revival Lupton Hall was built on the new campus, with an auditorium in its southwest end. The lovely old building also features a tower with a cast-bell carillon composed of forty-two resounding bells. These chime the quarter hours daily, adding an otherworldly feel to the campus. It is here that Dr. Brown's life in the theater unfolded, and it is here that his spirit prefers to visit.

Today the old Lupton Auditorium at Oglethorpe University is used mostly for student presentations, having been overshadowed in 1997 with the opening of the school's Conant Performing Arts Center. Still the old auditorium has the charm of yesteryear.

EXPERIENCING THIS GHOSTLY MANIFESTATION

Oglethorpe alumna and now instructor Lee Knippenberg is not certain that she believes in ghosts. She has long known of Dr. Brown's work at OU because her father had gone to school there after World War II. When she was herself an undergraduate there in 1980 and 1981, there was an annual award named after Dr. Brown given to the student who contributed the most to the theater at Oglethorpe.

Knippenberg recalls that when strange things began to happen in the auditorium in the early 1990s after she became a faculty member, she'd often remark that "Dr. Brown is visiting again!" She has since wondered if her rather flippant remarks, coupled with students' active imagination, have somehow "created" this ghost.

"For years, Wendell kept me and numerous students 'company' as we worked late into the night, putting the finishing touches on whatever show happened to be currently in production. Lights that were in perfect working order would suddenly malfunction and then, just as suddenly, function perfectly again. Windows would rattle and pop when there was no breeze. Doors would open and close unaided, tools would disappear and reappear, footsteps could be heard along the backstage corridor when the space was supposed to be empty. It all seemed to be Wendell's way of saying, 'I'm still here, and I'm on your side. I support what you do.'"

There are numerous specific manifestations of this spirit. Knippenberg shares one experience of a set of new stage lights that was not working properly, even

Haunted footsteps are occasionally heard late in the backstage corridor when the theater production crew works late into the night. Many believe the spirit of Dr. Wendell Brown is visiting his theater, just to check on things.

as late as the dress rehearsal just before the opening of a production. During rehearsals, half the lights would suddenly go out, and then come back on! She remembers telling the student actors that even if the lighting goes out, they were to continue the play, as if nothing was amiss, and the stage crew would bring the house lights up. She was terrified that everything would go wrong on the Thursday, Friday, Saturday, and Sunday afternoon performances of the show.

Much to her surprise, the lighting worked fine through every perform-ance. Still, just as they were taking down the set, they tested the lights for a concert that would be held soon thereafter, and all the problems appeared again. In Knippenberg's estimation, Dr. Brown was helping out. He doesn't want anything to go wrong with the performances, but is willing to show himself, as if to tease the actors and stage-hands during rehearsals.

Knippenberg and Dwyer both shared a specific experience of a locked door that was mysteriously unlocked at just the right time. Once in 1990, while a student was adjusting the side curtains on stage, the entire curtain and heavy support rod fell on his head. As the faculty member in charge, Knip-penberg immediately sent someone to the downstairs lounge to get some wet paper towels, since the head injury was bleeding profusely. Dwyer remembers that the door to the stairway was locked just prior to the accident, since there were soft-drink machines in the lounge and he'd tried just before the rehearsal to get a soda. Still a student soon produced the requested towels.

Knippenberg took the injured student to the hospital where he received fifteen or so stitches.

Dwyer returned to the auditorium about two hours after the accident to finish several tasks. He still wanted the soda, but he wasn't surprised to find that the door was still locked. It wasn't until several days later that Dwyer asked the student who retrieved the towels where he'd gotten them. The other student simply said downstairs. When Dwyer inquired further, the other student confirmed that the door leading to the downstairs lounge was unlocked when he went down right after the accident. The door was known to be locked fifteen minutes before the accident, unlocked just when it needed to be, and locked no more than two hours later. Of course, as Dwyer mentioned during our interview, campus security could have unlocked the door, and then locked it again less that 2 hours later. However, he considered that quite unlikely–after all, why would they do so when lights and students were still in the old auditorium? Dwyer believes, as does Knippenberg, that Dr. Brown managed to help them out that night yet again.

A GHOSTLY CEREMONY: MOVING THE SPIRIT

Oglethorpe faculty and students planned a celebration to mark the completion of the school's new performing arts center in 1997. Invitations were soon sent to alumni across the nation for the gala event. Someone suggested a ceremony to move Dr. Brown's spirit into the new theater space as one aspect of the festivities and, after some planning, a ceremony was devised to do just that. The ceremony was not merely a gimmick, but was taken quite seriously, as subsequent events were to demonstrate.

Originally the ceremony involved a procession across campus from the Lupton Auditorium to the arts center. However, the procession idea was nixed at the confidential request of a member of the faculty who worked in the new building--it seems he or she didn't particularly want a spirit moving in!

Also, Knippenberg recalls a warning from an alumna who confessed to being a "witch": the ceremony was treading on dangerous ground in attempting to move a spirit. Knippenberg remembers the conversation as a stern warning about trying to displace a ghost. For these reasons, a scaled down version of the original planned ceremony was held—complete with a "Moving the Spirit Ceremony" program. Knippenberg does report however that the ceremony seems to have been a failure. Manifestations are still associated only with Lupton, with nothing in the way of haunted experiences reported in the new performing arts center.

And the manifestations do continue today. Jessica DeMaria shared one example of a recent occurrence in Lupton. She arrived at Oglethorpe in 1998 and was very active in theater there until her graduation in 2002. In particular she was involved with the Shadowbox Players, a student-run theater group that used Lupton Auditorium for its performances, even after the new performance hall had been completed. DeMaria and a fellow cast member were getting the old auditorium ready for a performance one day in 1998, and remembered that a window backstage had been broken. They checked and confirmed that it was still covered over by plastic and tape and thus noise or cold would not be a problem during the performance. They then began cleaning up the backstage area, and while they worked, DeMaria told the story of Wendell the ghost....

"... and all of a sudden it started to get really cold; I know that sounds campy, because that's exactly what everybody says [about ghosts]," DeMaria says, "but it started to get really cold and we assumed it was the hole in the glass that we'd just checked. So we went back over there to check it out and it was fine—it was all taped up with no air coming through. Then, all of the lights went out, and we were just there in utter darkness. We were terrified, clutching at each other in the dark; hair was standing up on the back of my neck. Then the lights just went back on. It was a like a wake-up call: 'I'm still here; don't mess around!'"

Clearly, Dr. Brown had made his presence know again, this time as the kind of "cold spot" or "cold wind" that is a common manifestation of the spirits.

EVIDENCE OF THIS SPIRIT?

Interestingly Knippenberg did not demonstrate a strong belief in ghosts during our interview. Indeed, she wonders if her remarks somehow created the spirit. Thus, here is one witness of unexplained phenomena who can't state definitively that she believes in spirits. This challenging attitude towards the supernatural may, in fact, be evidence for these experiences in a sense, since it suggests something positive about Knippenberg's credibility.

Dwyer and DeMaria each seemed willing to express a "belief in something." Dwyer indicated a belief in "things unexplained or yet undiscovered." DeMaria shared with me several examples of ghostly manifestations she has experienced. She believes she is somehow sensitive to spiritual manifestations. Still, each of these witnesses is quite credible, in my view. I left each of these interviews convinced of the sincerity of these folks. Each is totally believable, and each is now employed by Oglethorpe University, suggesting that administrators on campus have vested serious responsibilities in each of these individuals, and value the contributions they make.

While the manifestations seem to be quite numerous, no actual image of Dr. Brown has ever been seen--as far as anyone today can determine. Still the examples presented above represent only a few of his manifestations. Clearly, this is a spirit that wants to be noticed, but the fact remains that this could be virtually any spirit at all!

With that uncertainty stated, the spirit seems to assist the theater program at every turn, adjusting lights, and assuring that things run smoothly during performances. He is a prankster only during rehearsals. For that reason, I am inclined to believe that Dr. Brown lingers here still. After all, that may only be expected from someone like this learned man, who loved his craft with such a passion and dedication. All of his students are enriched by his memory, by his love of drama, and by the joy he brought to generation after generation of students and faculty here.

Now we take our leave from Dr. Brown and his haunted auditorium, but not before thanking him for his contributions to theater and to the university, and wishing him well in his never-ending journey. The tribute paid to Dr. Brown by the current faculty and students at Oglethorpe is most fitting. In honor of his accomplishments in life, as well as in view of his spiritual visits, faculty and students reserve an empty seat for Dr. Brown at every theatrical performance. Dr. Brown always has one of the choicest seats—third row back—and this touching tradition continues today at Oglethorpe.

THE OLD OFFICERS CLUB AT DOBBINS

B e it an older couple materializing in the office or a younger girl manifesting in the entryway, one must conclude that the old Officers Club at Dobbins Air Force Base outside Atlanta is haunted. The club was located in a three-story wood and brick house built in the early 1800s and known originally as Cottage Hill. The home was also known as the Gardner Place, and records show a sale of the building as early as 1862. The building was erected on the original site of the Woodlawn Plantation and became the officers club in the around the 1950s. With this rich and varied history, one can only wonder at the ghostly manifestations in this old building. (Today, the building may be found on General Road on the grounds of Dobbins Air Force Base; it is used as an office building by Lockheed Aircraft Corporation and is not open to the public.)

This building is old, and speaks to one as one walks across its floor. There is a long history of hauntings here and the manifestations continue until this day. In 1984, Nick Joiner, a Lockheed Corporation employee, was unlocking the door of the building, and was shocked to see at the foot of the inside stairs an image of a young woman in her late twenties. Joiner reports that she paused at the foot of the stairs, and then began to "float upward." According to Arthur Myers' *The Ghostly Register,* approximately twenty different employees of Lockheed have experienced strange phenomena in the house over the years. One may only guess what types of manifestations may have occurred prior to the corporate office phase of the home's history.

Geneva Perry worked at the officers club in the 1970s. Once she was alone in the building on a Saturday morning when she heard the front door open and close. She reports that she subsequently left her office and went to see who had come in. Finding no one, she then returned to her desk, but in just a moment heard footsteps. When she looked up she saw a ghostly apparition of an elderly couple standing in the doorway, where they stayed for several minutes, then left the room, leaving her terrified and wondering who this couple might have been.

WHY IS THIS BUILDING STILL HERE?

When so many older buildings were destroyed by General Sherman in his infamous Civil War March to the Sea, one may well ask, how did this older home survive? Legend suggests that as Sherman's troops marched past, an Englishman who was living in the property had the gall to hang out a British flag. Sherman, it is said, was determined that there was no need for "troubles" with foreign powers (indeed the Confederacy nurtured the hope almost through the end of the war that England would enter the War Between the States on its side). At any rate, the house was spared when many others weren't. It is also said that with the fleeing Confederate soldiers all around undergoing Union bombardment, two servants were killed in the yard of the house during the last year of the war. Perhaps the violent deaths of these two people have lead to manifestations such as those witnessed to this day.

All that is certain about these spirits is their level of activity. As reported by Myer, these spirits are incredibly active. Air force security officers Art Cleveland and Earl Martin have often secured the building, turning off lights and locking doors after closing hours. They are frequently surprised to look into the upstairs rooms—rooms that were secured in their rounds only moments before—to find that lights been turned back on and doors unlocked and open. Martin reported that he once drove by and saw open an upstairs window which he knew to have been permanently nailed shut. When he went upstairs, he found the light on and the window still open. Others report furniture moving by itself in the upstairs portions of the house.

WHO ARE THE GHOSTS?

Myer reported in 1986 that no one had established any plausible identify for these active, restless spirits, but Dan Cox, executive director of the Marietta Museum of History, thinks he may have an answer that ties these spirits to Marietta's Kennesaw House. In the mid-nineteenth century, Dix and Louisa Fletcher lived in the exact spot where the old officers quarters is now located. According to Cox, while the Fletchers owned the hotel which later became the Kennesaw House, their plantation, called Woodlawn, was located where the building now stands. Cox reports that the clothes worn by the spectral man and woman in that location correspond to the clothes know to be often worn by Dix and Louisa Fletcher. Specifically, Cox reports that the female spirit in the old officers quarters is often reported to wear a taffeta dress, a favorite fabric of Louisa Fletcher; while the male spirit is most often seen in overalls, Dix Fletcher's preferred dress for work on his plantation. According to Cox—a man who is prone to dry laughter at himself, "To further enhance my insanity, I say that's Dix and Louisa Fletcher out there."

Could these two ghosts from the nearby Kennesaw House travel a bit? Perhaps spirits do manifest themselves in several different places, each of which they called home in life.

SPIRITS IN THE DEKALB COUNTY COURTHOUSE

The grey façade of the DeKalb County Courthouse in Decatur, Georgia, speaks of days gone by. There is a life-size sculpture of a middle-age couple sitting on a park bench on the building's front lawn, so realistic that they seem alive. They sit there, in attire from an earlier age, suggesting a slower, less frantic lifestyle. They come from a time when this venerable 1898 courthouse was one of the larger structures in this small community minutes from downtown Atlanta—it is now dwarfed by many taller buildings. History lovers are drawn to the museum that is now housed in the courthouse, and perhaps, to the spirits of many prisoners—now long dead--who haunt the old building. The manifestations are centered around the staircase at the west end of the building. These decrepit stairs are now closed off to the public, but here prisoners of yesteryear moved to and from court and many heard their death sentences pronounced within these halls. Prisoners were moved in shackles to prevent escape and some suggest that the spirits—and the chains—linger still.

In the historic DeKalb County Courthouse, the spirits of condemned prisoners still plead their innocence, long after they were hanged.

Leon Kitchens loves local history. He is quite knowledgeable about the history of DeKalb County and about the old courthouse itself. He was a longtime docent at the courthouse's museum and had shown numerous visitors around the building. By age seventy-five, Kitchens had stopped his volunteer work, but he did confirm the experience, documented in several different sources including Nancy Roberts and Price, of a museum guest who sensed and then confirmed the presence of several ghosts in the old courthouse building—the ghosts of condemned prisoners in chains.

THE REVEREND FINDS A SPIRITUAL VISITOR

In January 1995, Kitchens was doing his volunteer work for the museum and was expecting nothing out of the ordinary. He noticed the date, the thirteenth, was a Friday, but those superstitions seemed silly to him. He was aware that some of the museum staff didn't care to work in the courthouse alone, and he'd heard stories of "the sounds of footsteps" in certain areas of the building, but he wasn't interested in things of that nature. Rather, he focused on his enjoyable volunteer work, describing the many interesting museum exhibits to the various guests.

Kitchens recalls that around 3:30 in the afternoon of the thirteenth, a man came in with two women. He introduced himself as the Reverend David Venator, pastor of the Pilgrim Trinitarian Congregational Church of Boston. When

Kitchens asked if he could show the clergyman around, Rev. Venator reported that he could not move from the spot in which he stood just inside the museum doorway. He said he felt a "cold spot" and couldn't move his legs; the excited reverend explained that the cold was not from the air, but seemed to be coming from the building itself. He was standing right beside the door in the main room of the museum which lead to an unused stairway. At this point, Rev. Venator mentioned that he was psychic and that he felt that there were presences in the old courthouse; he soon recovered and Kitchens began the tour. After moving through one gallery, the reverend again became intensely aware of the spirits.

"There are three rooms on that floor," Kitchens explained, "and this man walked to one wall where the sword of Stephen Decatur was on display. He said that he felt a chill, and that someone was standing on the other side of the wall. He thought someone was trying to contact him because he was a psychic."

Kitchens knew that there was an old, closed-off stairway behind that wall, and that it had been the route that prisoners has used going to and from court. The stairs connected to a series of rooms behind the judges' benches. There was also a holding cell in the basement where prisoners at one time were often kept on court days, but the door to that stairway is never opened since the stairway is not part of the museum tour. Further, the reverend had moved through a couple of rooms since finding the "cold spot" and nevertheless indicated a wall that hid the same stairway. From the place where the reverend was standing, there was no obvious physical connection to the location of the first "cold spot" he'd detected only a few minutes before.

When Rev. Venator continued to show interest, Kitchens was more than happy to open the unused door and show him the stairs leading down to the holding cell. Once in the stairwell, Rev. Venator went down a few steps, then removed from his pocket a small gold chain with a plumb bob at the end. He held the end of the chain and swung the plumb bob in a circular motion for a few minutes. He indicated that this was how he could detect spirits.

The reverend then said, "There's someone coming down the stairs, and he's crying. He has his hands over his face, and he's crying. He says he's not guilty. I sense a spirit on the stairs a few feet away from me. There is a negative energy down here."

As Kitchens watched in amazement, the reverend's voice took on a somewhat different quality and he spoke haltingly. Now apparently repeating the words from the troubled spirit, the Reverend continued, "I was tried and found guilty of a crime I did not commit."

David Joyner reported on this haunting in an article in the *Atlanta Journal-Constitution*. Apparently, the Rev. Venator was subsequently able to "visit" the old courthouse using his gold chain and plumb bob from his residence in Boston. In this account, the reverend found a number of spirits in the old courthouse, all of whom were in the haunted stairwell on the west end of the building, and many appeared to be shackled in chains. Clearly, at least one, and perhaps several spirits still wander these unused hallways. Further, these spirits are available for "remote detection" should a physic wish to establish such contact with them.

UNCERTAIN CONCLUSIONS:
INVESTIGATING THE STORY

When I contacted Kitchens in 2003, he was more than willing to confirm the story. A spokesman for the Pilgrim Congregational Church in Boston had known the Reverend Venator (who had died a few years after his experiences the courthouse) for a brief time. He confirmed that Rev. Venator had indeed been a minister at that church as well as a psychic. However, at this investigative dead end, we can move no further to investigate this haunting.

While there have been other reports from various workers of some "energy" in this area of the old courthouse, the haunting above is certainly the best documented. Some staff members report hearing footsteps or getting a feeling that they were not alone, even though no one else is in the building. However, finding sources for these stories has proven difficult, and when I visited the old courthouse, there was no one currently working there who could share any haunted experiences.

Still, the question remains: Absent a spiritual encounter, how did Rev. Venator know of the unused stairwell? With all the many stairways in the courthouse, why did the reverend single out this blocked-off, long-unused one—hidden from view behind a wall—and locate it twice as the source of spiritual energy? It would seem that the spirits wander still, in chains, as they move toward their haunted destiny in this hallowed court of law.

THE CHURCH THAT IS NO MORE
THE GHOSTS AT GEORGIA TECH

University campuses quite often overgrow some part of the cities that host them and the Georgia Institute of Technology is no exception. This forces the question, as a university annexes its surrounding neighborhoods, do the ghosts of any particularly haunted location then begin a collegiate career?

As the campus of Georgia Tech grew, it took in numerous landmarks and historic sites from the northwest part of the old city. During the Civil War part of the present-day campus was a battle line, the main Confederate defensive line northwest of the city. Numerous photos are available of some of the defenses built by the Confederates during the war, and Tech sits astride several batteries of the 1864 defensive line. More recently, homes occupied the spot, along with local stores and at least one church. Of course, as Tech has grown both physically and into one of the preeminent technological institutions in the nation, it has subsumed ever larger portions of the city.

The old Church of Christ building once stood on old Hemphill Avenue. By many accounts an ugly building, the front façade of the old church sported a three-door entrance and boarded-up, tall windows. According to a cornerstone that once stood at its entrance, the building was "rebuilt in 1940" on its Hemphill location. It was used as a church for a generation, then taken over by Georgia Tech, and finally used by Tech's student theater group DramaTech. In time, it was torn down, but not before the ghostly sounds of children were reported in the darkened hallways.

The manifestations, when experienced in the 1960s, were widely discussed at Georgia Tech. For example, Garland Humphries, once the publicity director for DramaTech, was very cautious about the building. He felt it to be an "evil place," and often stated that he would not stay alone in the building at night.

These spirits revealed themselves in various ways. A number of persons reported that they heard a heavy door that once stood at the end of the central hallway open and shut by itself, and that the voices of children—both loud and somewhat muffled-could be heard in the hallway outside of the theater offices. The voices seemed to move up and down past the door, as if the children were running and playing along the long expanse of hallway. The sound of heavy furniture being moved was also reported by journalist Judy Allen in *Atlanta* magazine. In her account, that spectral sound seemed to come from the first floor of the church, yet all who reported hearing those noises confirmed that they never found furniture out of place. On one occasion, a light was reported to have come on for no reason and was presumed to be a manifestation of this haunting.

In one instance, another executive of the drama group heard the ghostly children at play. He didn't believe in ghosts, and he knew that children were not allowed in the theater—props and sets can be dangerous things when used as children's playthings. Assuming at that point that the children were merely neighborhood kids who had somehow gotten past the locked door, he became concerned and actually left his office for the hallway to chase the trespassers away. Needless to say, in spite of having heard the children very distinctly, once he entered the hall, he found no one.

Some investigation of the phenomena was done in the 1960s. Allen indicates that several members of the theater group contacted the Church of Christ congregation at its new sanctuary across town to ascertain if there had ever been a tragedy involving a group of children at the church on Hemphill Avenue, but no church member could report any memory of such a tragedy. Further, the word *rebuilt* on the old cornerstone didn't bespeak of any difficulties experienced by the church, but rather of a simple location change to the site on Hemphill Avenue.

At long last, the old Church of Christ was torn down, and since that time no information on any haunting has been reported from that location. Apparently, with their old church and congregation gone, the spectral children of Georgia Tech have moved on.

THE GHOSTS OF THE NEWEL POSTS
AN IMPORTED SPIRIT ARRIVES IN ATLANTA

Kara O'Brien knew the monastery from which these two particular newel posts came was supposedly haunted; it was known as one of the most haunted sites in the whole country—but the posts seemed to be just right for the house she and her partner were fixing up together in northeast Atlanta. O'Brien wasn't overly concerned with ghosts or spirits—her parents lived in house in the lush Shenandoah Valley near a Civil War battlefield in Virginia that was haunted; she was raised with ghosts and was used to them. Besides, the heart pine newel posts were just perfect, exactly what her new house needed.

When the DeSales Heights Academy in Parkersburg, West Virginia, was torn down in 2002, a number of the pieces of woodwork became available for sale and were offered to dealers around the nation. As a dealer in antique woodwork herself and the co-owner of a business that restores older buildings throughout Atlanta—Laughing Sun Renovations— O'Brien has excellent insight into the value of fine craftsmanship. Her work is highly regarded, and some of her restorations have been featured in *This Old House* magazine. She often buys antique mantels, doors and doorframes, stained glass, and ornate woodwork from various sales around the country, typically finding what she needs for a particular restoration job either through dealers in Atlanta or over the internet. Her basement holds quite a collection of architectural salvage pieces that any lover of fine craftsmanship would enjoy.

When O'Brien found these particular newel posts in West Virginia, she purchased them in spite of some reservations. The dealer who sold them to her indicated that they had come from what he described as a "haunted monastery." Indeed, that these pieces had been blessed with holy water before they were sold to remove any possibility that spirits would associate themselves with the newel posts. Of course, this captured O'Brien's interest, and since they matched exactly what she and her partner had planned for the stairs in a house on Warlick Place, she bought then. She anticipated using one for the stairs into the basement, and one for the stairs leading to the second floor.

The house itself is a two-story structure that had originally been built by Frank Ruggles (see his own story in this book, "A Haunting in Kirkwood: Mr. Ruggles Comes Home"), and as such it had a number of unique features. Unlike the original Ruggles home, this house had been redesigned many times, and was in horrible condition when O'Brien purchased it. Still, much of the original beauty was evident, merely covered over with layers of paint and grime during the last century. Much of Ruggles's other work was there—stained glass, wood columns, and leaded glass windows. Ruggles houses are known for beautiful woodwork and in remodeling this house, O'Brien wanted to find just the right piece for each stairway, window, and door. Little did she realize that she was importing spirits along with these distinctive examples of West Virginia woodwork.

GHOSTLY FACES AND FLOATING ORBS

A spirit, by all indications, entered the house on Warlick Place just when the newel posts arrived. When O'Brien first took the newel posts to her own home, even prior to even unloading these pieces of turned and carved wood, she took a couple of pictures of them in the back of her sport utility vehicle. She was aware of the rumors of hauntings at DeSales Heights and after taking the pictures, she decided to invite the ghost to show himself, should there be one attached to these pieces of wood.

"It was so weird because I took six pictures from that exact spot, and it wasn't until I said, "If there's a ghost would you please present yourself on my film.' And I took it, and immediately when I took it, I said, 'I got something! But I don't know what I've got.' When we came back here, we looked at it and saw a very clear image."

O'Brien got very excited by the orbs. She understood that a number of researchers in the paranormal believe that spirits captured on film often show up as orbs of light. O'Brien was aware both of the possible meaning of these orbs, and of the legend suggesting that the monastery from which these newel posts came was haunted. Her roommate was much less enthusiastic about the orbs, and then, just by chance they noticed the small ghostly face captured on the window of the SUV in the same photograph. In fact, upon close examination, the face seems to be that of a man with the shaved head of a monk, and there appears to be a small cross over the face. Based on that picture, each was convinced they had imported a West Virginia spirit. None of the other five pictures taken from the same spot show the face—apparently this spirit prefers an invitation prior to such a manifestation.

A HAUNTED MONASTERY

The DeSales Heights Academy sat on a prominent hill in Parkersburg West Virginia, for over a hundred and thirty-eight years, and if any location in the United States has a right to be haunted, it was this old building. Originally, eight nuns from the order of the Sisters of the Visitation came to Parkersburg in 1864, the final full year of the Civil War. The sisters opened the first girl's school in the area atop a hill overlooking the growing town. The nuns dressed in ancient attire and, by all accounts, caused quite a stir in this rugged mountain community; this town had, quite simply, never seen women of such determination before. The convent was located next door to a saloon which attracted a rather raucous clientele, and this caused the sisters considerable concern early on. Still, the sisters established a Catholic girls' boarding school and a school for the poorer children of the town. Eventually a monastery was also built on a hill overlooking Parkersburg and the Ohio River. While the interior of the academic building was quite plain, the DeSales Heights Academy included a magnificent chapel with an altar carved from beautiful Italian marble. The school was soon known for excellence, and pupils arrived from all over the eastern United States; the name DeSales Heights became famous for producing young ladies of culture who would be leaders in their communities. Moreover, many daughters of the heads of state of Central and South American countries were sent to DeSales Heights for their educations.

In spite of this fame DeSales Heights also became known for ghosts over the years. There is the legend that the eight original sisters were buried in a basement hallway, and that could give rise to spirits in the old school. These spirits were investigated by the West Virginia Ghost Hunters before the building was torn down. Furthermore, many children died while receiving their education there, given the primitive medical conditions in the 1800s and early 1900s. There are reports of a murder of a small child that took place during the long histories of the monastery and school. In fact, that haunting seems particularly well documented. For example, the website of the West Virginia

One can see the orb just above the floor near the wall by the stairway. This stairway is where one of the haunted newel posts has been installed. Do orbs such as these represent imported spirits?

Ghost Hunters has a number of photos of floating orbs from DeSales Heights, as well as several pictures of "faces in windows." Thus, the pictures O'Brien took seem hauntingly reminiscent of the West Virginia pictures.

As participation in Catholic monastic life declined beginnings in the 1960s, fewer children were in attendance at the academy. In March 1991, after 138 years of service, the order announced that it would no longer be able to continue its educational duties. By the end of 1992, the hallways fell silent forever, leaving only the occasional spiritual manifestation, a whisper of ghostly feet in the hallway above the bodies of the original eight nuns, or sounds of a dying child crying. By 2001, the building had been heavily vandalized, making the decision to destroy the building easier. West Virginians of many faiths mourned the loss of this important piece of Mountain State history.

ORBS OF OTHER GHOSTS?

The manifestations of this imported spirit (or is it spirits?) have only increased over time. O'Brien spent time investigating the spirits in the old DeSales Heights Academy, and became acquainted with the theory that the orbs which appear in photographs of haunted locations represent the "nucleus of spirits." As a result of her investigations, she was convinced that a spirit attached to the newel posts now resided in her house on Warlick Place. In sharing this interesting story of the haunted newel posts with friends one evening, O'Brien suddenly realized that she had hundreds of pictures of older buildings that she had renovated. In fact, she used these pictures as "before and after renovation" photos that could guide her in her work on a particular house. She thought that this might be a rich treasure of photos of similar orbs. When looking at the pictures from the house at Warlick Place taken in May 2002, she found a photograph that showed a couple of orbs in the dining room, as well as a couple of orbs in the area around the mantel in the smoking room. These photos were taken in the house right after it was purchased by O'Brien, and before the newel posts were even purchased!"orbs in dinning room"]

MANIFESTATIONS OF THE SPIRITS

While photos of orbs are intriguing, there are other manifestations in the house. Doors are frequently heard to shut for no apparent reason. Generally this takes place in the back hall, and on some occasions the doors literally slam shut with a bang. Frequently, this happens in the middle of the night. Also, on one occasion when O'Brien and her roommate returned from a trip, they found the back bedroom door unlocked. They were certain they had locked it prior to leaving. There seems to be a never-ending stream of sounds from the hallway on the west side of the main floor of the home. O'Brien indicated that the newel posts were stored there for a time, prior to being installed on the stairways in the house, and she believes that the spirits may have preferred the hallway, since so many noises seemed to be heard in that area. On one occasion, while O'Brien and her roommate were away for Christmas in 2002, their dogsitter came to check the pets that had been left in the doghouse outside, and heard the horn of their SUV going off nonstop. He joggled the horn and it stopped easily; it has never given them trouble since.

O'Brien reports that one of her three dogs has noticeda spirit in O'Brien's bedroom. "One time, the dog started acting weird. She was in her bed and all of a sudden she started seeing things moving around the floor. Her head was jerking like it was something moving really fast. One night—the first night we had the newel posts in the house—she wouldn't go to sleep. She kept getting out of her bed, and going and standing behind the bed and just watching something. She was sending chills up and down my spine, because she was seeing something or hearing something that we didn't. Her ears were going crazy."

O'Brien further reports that there have been several other nights such as that one, but that the first night the newel posts were in the house was the worst. On that night the dog would not go to sleep for hours, whereas that pet had always drifted to sleep quite easily before.

I asked the two when these manifestations began. They reported that they had only been in the house since May 2002. Neither reported that they had any experiences of this nature before the newel posts arrived, but again several pictures taken prior to the arrival of the newel posts in the initial renovation, did show several orbs. Perhaps there were a number of reasonably quite ghosts in this home prior to the arrival of the spirits of the newel posts.

RELIABLE WITNESSES?

As in most of the stories I've investigated, these two people seem completely reliable as witnesses for these manifestations. These are business partners and close friends who manage a sizable remodeling crew ranging from twelve to fifteen full-time people that has grown into a successful business in the last several years, suggesting overall stability as well as significant people skills. Interestingly, while both now believe in ghosts, they have quite a different reaction to them. While O'Brien reports being "freaked out," by ghosts, her partner (who wishes to remain nameless) does not report being particularly frightened.

While I managed to uncover several spirits in Atlanta and Athens that apparently travel from one nearby location to another, this is the only example of an imported spirit that I've found in Atlanta. Further, with the destruction of the DeSales Heights Academy, there would appear to be very little investigation possible on who this spirit (or spirits) may be. I can only assure the reader that these two homeowners are earnest in their belief that they reside with one or more specters in a beautifully restored home on Warlick Place. Further, these two are highly accomplished, and successful people, each of whom is completely believable as a witness to such an unexplained ghostly manifestation. Perhaps in the future, more pictures of these spirits will shed light on whatever unfinished business they may have in their newfound home in our fair city.

SPIRITS IN THE DUNWOODY FARMHOUSE

Linda had taken a great deal of kidding from her husband David about her belief that their unique old farmhouse in Dunwoody was haunted, that is until, according to Linda, "he saw the Bible rise from the table, hover, and then drop to the floor nearby." The Bible, a generations-old family heirloom, has been observed to move by itself at least three times, and even when it doesn't levitate, it is rarely found in the same spot where it was last laid by human hands.

This isn't the only evidence of a spirit in this old home. There are times when the light fixture in the dining room flickers during the evening meal. While electricians have searched and searched, nothing can be found to cause this flickering of the lights. Now, when it flickers during a meal, David merely yells at it and it stops flickering

A ghostly face—the face of an old woman with her hair pulled back—is often seen in one of the upstairs bedroom windows, towards the front of the house.

The Dunwoody farmhouse (ca. 1870).

Linda and many of her guests have seen this particular manifestation. The old woman wears a dress with a high collar, in a style popular around 1890. There is no clear indication of who this spirit may be, except for the fact that some former owners once told David that the bedroom in the right front was called the "birthing room." It was common many years ago to identify a specific room in a home as a room for giving birth to children. Often, this would have been a room known for either its warmth or its afternoon sunshine, and the room on the right front of the old home does indeed face toward the southwest into the afternoon sun.

FAMOUS SPIRITS

Perhaps the most famous haunted house in Atlanta, the farmhouse is on the corner of Vermack and Chamblee-Dunwoody Road, just inside the perimeter in northeast Atlanta. The manifestations suggest that at least three spirits inhabit the old farmhouse, and these ghosts are now famous. This haunting has been reported in numerous books and magazines and because of the "fame" of this haunting, I really didn't know what to expect when I talked with the current homeowners—David, a well-respected attorney who played in the yard of the farmhouse as a child, and Linda, an interior decorator and instructor of historic renovation with longstanding ties to the area. However, it quickly became apparent that they were used to discussing these spirits and there was no nervousness about their resident ghosts. Further, the more one gets to know about David and Linda, the more it becomes clear that they are reliable, well-respected members of the community. These are not people one would normally associate with spirits.

HISTORY OF THE OLD FARMHOUSE

Returning from the Civil War, farmer W. J. Donaldson purchased a fairly large track of land stretching from Dunwoody to Chamblee and, in 1870, built his house and a number of outbuildings there. He married three times, outliving each wife, until his death in 1900. Donaldson's last wife, Adeline, survived him and remained in the farmhouse until her death in the mid 1930s. This is one reason that the front and oldest portion of the house is preserved in the original plain plantation style—two rooms downstairs, two up, and a connecting stairway between the two floors. Many such buildings harbor spirits, perhaps because of the age of this type of house.

The farm was divided among his heirs after Adeline's death, and, over the years, a number of larger rooms have been added to the rear of the structure, but the old farmhouse remains a fixture of the community. Now surrounded by suburban homes, this house--along with several others on the Chamblee-Dunwoody Road—preserve a rich sense of the history of this area.

David and Linda toured the property in 1975 prior to their decision to purchase it. There was no heat in the house and the weather was cold, but in spite of that, Linda felt a presence in the home. "We knew there was something there, " she says. They did not feel uneasy at all, and if anything, were more determined to purchase the historic old home after that visit.

THE SPIRITUAL MANIFESTATIONS

Many spiritual manifestations are reported in the old farmhouse. For example, overnight guests often report hearing faintly the sounds of a choir in one of the rooms in the older part of the house. That room is called the Parson's Room because many visiting ministers have stayed in that room when traveling through.

There is also the story of a reporter and his television crew who wished to investigate the hauntings in the old home. A reporter from an Atlanta television station asked to spend Halloween night in the old farmhouse. He brought along a psychic and a cameraperson for the evening. The crew believed that they saw two spirits hovering in the yard near the old family cemetery located slightly to the northeast of the old house. However, when the cameraman tried to film the apparitions, the cameras would not work. These cameras had been checked earlier in the day and were then working perfectly.

The psychic stated that there was a great deal of supernatural activity within the home, but that the spirits didn't want to be captured on videotape. The cameraman, however, reacted quite negatively to the equipment failure, and was so nervous that he refused to sleep in the house that Halloween night.

By numerous reports, however, these spirits are not, by and large, scary specters. In fact Linda believes that these ghosts may have saved their lives one evening in 1998. In March of that year, a tornado ripped through the northern suburbs of Atlanta and demolished many older buildings. The family had heard the warnings of severe thunderstorms, but assumed that the rain presented no real threat. Each member of the family was sleeping soundly when they were awakened just after midnight by a raging storm and decided to retreat to the storm cellar.

David and Linda both headed downstairs, with Linda delayed just a bit to retrieve their pet dog. The family didn't follow their usual route out of the house, but instead were led through the darkness and out a different backdoor by one of the spirits. As they were leaving, the raging wind uprooted two old trees that crashed through the house's upper floor. The family would have been crushed by these trees had they exited the house as they usually did. Linda states this belief very confidently: "The spirits guided us."

INVESTIGATIONS OF THIS HAUNTING

Researchers explore ghostly manifestations in various ways. Journalist Mickey Goodman chose to use a psychic to investigate this house. He had her "visualize" the property prior to her visit. The psychic agreed to meditate on the house, try to determine any facts about it, and gauge the psychic activity there. As she meditated, she identified several things. She drew a floor plan and identified the upstairs rear bedroom as the scene of most of the psychic activity (interestingly not the birthing room). Goodman reports that "she 'saw' a tall, thin old man who . . . roamed the halls with a woman who was good at making pickles, as well as a small girl, perhaps named Lou Ann. She described a closet that had been added when the stairwell was moved during remodeling, and she felt strongly that someone had been shot in the house and on the property, perhaps during the Civil War. The scents of Irish oatmeal and pickling spices were present and she picked up the letter *L* in addition to the names Frank and Harry Stevens."

The psychic was amazingly accurate in a number of particulars. In fact, Goodman identifies a number of "hits" in the information above.

The homeowners confirmed the story of the couple and the young girl. The stairwell had, indeed, been moved to face the rear of the house and in space beneath it, a coat closet had been added. Linda and her daughter also confirmed poltergeist-like experiences in the rear bedroom, such as finding money scattered about the room, as well as spirits that often wandered about the upstairs hall and the entry hall near the stairwell. Although Linda has never been able to corroborate it, local lore persists about a shooting in the downstairs bedroom during a family dispute.

It is likely that a Civil War skirmish or two took place on the property because a Union encampment was located just down the road. One of the home's previous owners was named Frank, and Harry Stevens might have been one of the numerous tenant farmers who worked the land. Also, when the family moved into the house, they found a number of pickling jars. Linda remembered that the woman from whom they purchased the house was named Lois, making the *L* connection.

Linda and David corroborated several of psychic's findings as factually correct aspects of the house's history, including the ghost couple and young girl; an original stairway having been moved during remodeling and a closet built beneath the new stair; the rear bedroom as the center of psychic activity; the strong possibility of the shooting of a soldier during a Civil War skirmish there;

the pickle jars, the name "Frank" as that of a previous owner, and the connection of a former owner with the letter *L*.

However, the psychic had no visions of flickering lights, a singing choir, the old woman in the front bedroom, or levitating bibles. Such is the stuff of psychic exploration. While this evidence is certainly impressive, it is not conclusive.

With that concern noted, this is still a most impressive combination of evidence and may suggest a high level of activity in this old farmhouse. In this famous haunting, we have levitation of objects, spiritual guidance, physical manifestations, and reports of some interesting facts from psychics.

Here we leave Atlanta's most famous spiritual manifestation. The accounts of this haunting will certainly continue, given the high profile of this manifestation. Perhaps in the future we'll learn more about these spirits, who they are, how they lived, how they died, and what came afterward. I'd certainly love the opportunity to question them as we begin to understand more of the nature of hauntings such as these.

A GHOST IN SOUTHWEST ATLANTA?

There have been many reports of a haunting in an older house in southeast Atlanta during the 1960s. This spirit was apparently quite active both during the day and in the evenings. During the day, various small objects—books, keys, and such—would seemingly vanish and then reappear in other places. Mary, the single mother of two daughters, would place her keys and pocketbook down on a table near the door when she came home, and either or both would be found a hour later under the desk in the middle of the bedroom. Mary and her children also heard music coming from the kitchen, where there was no radio or other source of music.

The house itself is an older bungalow in a typical suburban neighborhood near Fort McPherson. The warm, cozy bungalow has a large living room, as well as three bedrooms, a den, a kitchen, and a large basement. One descends to the basement either by the outside stairs or the stairway, which connected it to one of the bedrooms. Only one side of the basement was finished, and a wall separated that side from the other, which still had a dirt floor. In short, this was a typical house for that neighborhood of Atlanta; of course, is any residence with ghosts typical?

THE SPIRIT IS SURPRISED

One time, Mary was down in the finished side of the basement. She knew her daughters were away; still she heard sounds of footsteps moving overhead. She also heard drawers being opened in the bedroom, as well as the sound of water running in the bathroom. Investigating these sounds by going upstairs, Mary found nothing—no drawers opened; no water running.

Mary reported that this was not an isolated occurrence. In fact, many afternoon naps were disturbed by this spirit. The manifestations involved an unseen presence coming into the house and walking about, running water, and even—on one occasion— flushing the toilet. This specter became quite distracting. Mary remembered that once she sat up and yelled at the ghost to go away. Mary then heard a male voice say, "She can see me!"

Every member of the family was having unusual experiences. For example, Mary's oldest daughter heard the sounds of a typewriter in the basement. She knew that there was no typewriter there, and realized she was hearing something unearthly. While still in bed one morning, Mary heard two sets of footsteps—the quick pitter-patter of a child and the heavier steps of an adult. This suggests that several spirits inhabit this home. One set of footsteps seemed to move into her younger daughter's room. The adult footsteps came down the hall, through the bedroom door, and seemed to stop at the foot of Mary's bed. One many only imagine how Mary felt, lying on the bed, listening to footsteps come her way!

SOUNDS IN THE DARKNESS:
THE TOUCH OF A GHOST

The manifestations, if anything, were even more scary at night. Once, in 1962 at two o'clock in the morning, the family heard someone trying to break in the front door. The next night it happened again, and soon became a nightly occurrence for a period of time. When Mary and her daughters looked, they never found any marks on the door or the surrounding doorframe. Something was making noises as if they were breaking in, but leaving no evidence of any attempt to do so.

On another occasion, late in the evening, Mary heard someone digging in the dirt floor in the unfinished side of the basement below the bedrooms. One may only speculate on what use the spirits may have planned for the hole beneath the house. This sound too, continued night after night, and each morning as the family investigated there was never any sign of disturbed dirt.

Perhaps the most terrifying occurrence involved the touch of a ghost. Both Mary and her youngest daughter shared this experience. Each reported one evening that it seemed as if a ghostly, ice-cold hand had touched them while they slept, as if to awaken them. This was terrifying. The youngest daughter thought she saw a shadowy form near her bed after she was awakened by the hands, but Mary did not report any notice of such a figure.

A PSYCHIC RESCUE, AND A PRAYER

Mary had always known she had some degree of psychic abilities. She was determined, after a few months of these phenomena, to try to make contact with the spirit or spirits. First, she relaxed deeply in an effort to seek the entities in the house. She wanted to find out why this haunting was taking place. At first, she heard a female voice—the voice of a ghost—say very clearly, "I need your help." Mary asked out loud, "Where are you?" The specter answered that she was in the basement.

Mary soon invited several friends over to try and help the spirit by conducting a "psychic rescue." However, it seems that the spirit was only interested in talking with Mary, and the rescue didn't have any impact on the manifestations at all.

After that, Mary again heard the pleading voice invite her to the basement. At that point, Mary was quite desperate, so she went down to the basement alone, with the intention of helping the specter if she could. When she got to the finished side of the basement, Mary didn't really know what to do; in desperation, she got down on her knees and began a very long prayer for these restless spirits.

Apparently, it worked! Perhaps the psychic rescue and the prayer and were enough to convince these spirits that they were indeed deceased. Perhaps the prayer resulted in unseen help for other worldly sources. At any rate, the manifestations stopped after the prayer, and Mary and her daughters were troubled no more.

I should note that I have found only one account of this haunting, and it didn't provide any information for a possible follow-up. For example, neither the full names of those involved nor an actual address, were given. Thus, this interesting story is reported here as representative of numerous legends of hauntings in Atlanta that defy further investigation.

III

RUMORS OF ATLANTA SPIRITS

In many cases, spirits, ghosts, or specters show themselves only tentatively. In some cases, as the following examples suggest, one can be hard-pressed to determine if there is indeed any evidence of a true haunting. For example, when spirits of deceased relatives appear in dreams, does that suggest a true haunting or an emotional need for closure on the part of the living? This is the central question in the story of "Her Father's Visits in Lake Claire."

However, this conundrum takes on another more interesting form when spirits who appear in dreams are unknown to the living. In some cases these "dream spirits" seem to bring information to the living that he or she could not have known otherwise. This seems to have been the case in the story of the "Missionary Spirits Who Need A Home." Frankly, I found the experience of investigating and documenting that story to be especially interesting because the spirits seemed to be investigating *me*. I felt the presence of something from beyond even before my first telephone contact with the women who had experienced the hauntings. Before the end of this conversation, not only were my personal beliefs examined, but my commitment to this book and to the "cause" of haunted spirits generally was challenged in a quite unusual way.

Still, these specters—f indeed they are—are somewhat less documented than the other spirits presented herein. Stories in this section, such as "Faces in the Windows," are also more emotionally demanding, You will sense and feel the emotional pull of these rumored spirits.

With these concerns stated, these spirits were reported to me by completely trustworthy and successfully functioning individuals in Atlanta. In each case, I found that I trusted these witnesses who shared openly and honestly their understanding of "dream spirits" or "uneasy feelings." So I give this collections of stories for the reader's consideration. Read these and then ask yourself, "Have I ever dreamed I talked to a deceased relative? Did I?"

MISSIONARY SPIRITS WHO NEED A HOME

After retrieving a message from her on my office voice mail, I returned a call to a Teri Stewart, who asked several probing questions concerning my experiences with hauntings and my beliefs on ghosts. I had not circulated a phone number for this book project and thought it a bit strange to receive this call at the university. Thus, I was a bit cautious about this contact, but I'd gotten used to such questions since many individuals with stories to share seek reassurance that their experiences will be handled with respect and not ridicule. I reviewed briefly with the caller that my beliefs had changed during the writing of this book; that I had moved from a position of suspended disbelief to a certainty that these phenomenon exist.

I further assured my questioner that I intended to handle each haunting shared with me with reverent respect—that I didn't "hunt" ghosts using cameras, gravity meters, or other scientific equipment; and that I didn't "clean" houses or try to rid locations of their resident spirits. It was not unusual that someone wishing to share a story with me would want to ascertain that I would respect their experiences, and in fact, Stewart indicated that this discussion had made her quite comfortable with my beliefs. She then proceeded to make me extremely uncomfortable, while at the same time, quite intrigued.

Stewart asked if I was Christian, and while I'd not been asked that question in preparation of this book, I told her I was and didn't see any conflict between my religious beliefs and my exploration of true ghost stories. Her next question, however, startled me completely; she asked if I was by any chance Presbyterian. This stunned me because I thought there was no way for her to know of my lifelong Presbyterian background.

I told Stewart that I had indeed been raised a Presbyterian and had attended St. Andrews Presbyterian College as an undergraduate many years ago. About ten years ago, my wife and I sought and found a Baptist church that met our needs and moved to that church. However, that decision had been somewhat painful for me, since I had been Presbyterian essentially all of my life.

Further, I was not sure how Stewart would have known that, nor did I see why she was curious. In my shock, I asked her about her questions, and she simply said that two of her resident spirits had insisted that she call me and ask that. Again, I was stunned! Apparently, these specters were having her check me out!

Then I began to consider possibilities. Of course, I had invited many neighborhood associations to "spread the word" that I was looking for true hauntings in the greater Atlanta area, and I assumed that Stewart contacted me because of one of those invitations. That information stated that I was a university professor, and armed with that fact, she could have accessed my vita posted on my university's website, and noted that I had attended a Presbyterian college. She later confirmed that she had received word from one of those neighborhood associations about this project, but that she had not looked up my credentials in that fashion.

When I interviewed her a few days later, she insisted that these two spirits had made her pursue this contact with me. For my part, I had never had a spirit seek me out. By the end of the thirty-minute phone conversation, I was in relative shock at Stewart's story.

Stewart believes she lives with three human spirits and two animal spirits. She feels that the three spirits were happy and felt they were in an appropriate home.

The spirits of two Presbyterian missionaries likewise lived with Stewart and had insisted to her that she place a call to me based on my e-mail to her neighborhood association. Those two spirits—who revealed their names to her as Johnson—wanted the story of their decades of missionary work told and they believed I might be the one to do it. Stewart had acquired them when she rescued two old steamer trunks from the garbage. The spirits were living in the trunks and needed a more appropriate home. Stewart finally inquired if I would be willing to talk to these spirits and assist them in telling their story.

Of course, I had never had such a request, and told her I would consider it, but that I couldn't make such a decision immediately. That request still sends shivers down my spine as I write this. While my beliefs had expanded considerably in writing this book, I'd had only one experience that I considered actual participation in a haunting up to that point—I'd smelled the ghost in the Eagle Tavern in Watkinsville, Georgia. Other than that one experience, I have had no direct experience with hauntings at all. Did I really want possession of two missionary spirits? As I write this, I note with amusement my inadvertent selection of that term, "possession." If I did take these two spirits to live with me, who would possess whom?

A DELIGHTFUL VISIT

With some trepidation, I met with Stewart the following week. I tried to have no preconceived notions, though I certainly failed in that regard. Any and every possibility seemed to come up in my mind, some of them quite frightening, and I was nervous right up to the minute that I met her.

I shouldn't have been concerned. Stewart is a delight, eccentric in a wonderfully creative way, quite well spoken, thoroughly knowledgeable in spiritual matters, artistic, highly creative, and pleasingly unconventional. She is a straightforward person, who looks her visitors straight in the eye, quite intensely. Within minutes, one feels comfortable around her, and that is her true gift.

Built in 1912, the single-story house on Gordon Avenue is laid out in a rather unusual plan—rooms seem to ramble one into another, but the whole puts one at ease. She has an expansive collection of unusual art work, interesting artifacts, and wonderful antiques. Her small front yard features a charming cottage garden.

Concerning her spirits, Stewart explains, "I don't know whether 'ghosts' is the appropriate term. I tend to think of them as generally benevolent spirits. Sometimes a bit mischievous," Stewart explained.

"The Johnsons are Arnold and Betty, who were very well-known missionaries in China from the 1920s to the 1950s. They called themselves "A" and "B." They have very different personalities. Arnold is much more patriarchal and pushy; Betty tends to be more complaining and a perfectionist. They've been here with me for a year."

COLLECTING THE SPIRITS

S tewart uses anything and everything in her artistic endeavors. She operates a small workshop that recycles garbage into artwork. While collecting materials for her art projects one afternoon, she and a friend noted several steamer trunks and some other objects sitting by the curb to be collected with the garbage. Stewart stopped immediately and picked over the pile of garbage. The trunks held an incredible assortment of Asian antiques, including some hand-painted silk tapestries, several of which she imagined to be quite valuable. Prior to taking them, she decided to inform the homeowners that some of the objects were, in her opinion, quite valuable.

Can these steamer trunks contain the spirits of long-dead missionaries?

They said that they really didn't care, and that Stewart should just take whatever items she wanted, which she did with glee. When she later went through one of the trunks— the one who belonged to Reverend Johnson, she was astounded at the historical treasurers it contained. Srewart found a tremendous amount of personal letters, bills, drawings, immunization records, and family photos. She put the

118

personal items aside. She then realized that the trunk had a false bottom and she recovered even more personal items—the Johnsons' personal treasures from a lifetime. She found Rev. Johnson's own Bible, one that he used from 1920 through 1950 in China and Taiwan, with his initials and last name embossed into the cover. Mrs. Johnson's wire-rimmed glasses were in the trunk, along with pictures of the missionaries in old age. The trunk included a piece of marble that was labeled "The Acropolis, 1929" which had obviously been chipped from that world-famous Greek temple when tourists still did such things.

Stewart realized that she'd uncovered an entire family history. She felt that she held in her hands the very "lives of these people," as she described it, and she could not imagine that this stuff was put on the curb intentionally.

"Two of the most precious things are the journal of Arnold's mother," Stewart explained. "which was done in 1870 during Reconstruction. It is her clippings, her poetry, her writings, with some Confederate money in there. It also held his mother's leather-bound autograph book dating from the 1870s."

The reverend's family owned a plantation on Amelia Island that was burned during the Civil War, and the reverend had obviously treasured these memoirs, judiciously safeguarding them throughout a lifetime of travel. Stewart couldn't imagine discarding these items with the garbage, though, of course, she did not immediately realize that she had acquired spirits with the collection. Also, one may only imagine the spirits being somewhat angry at this treatment of their lives and their history.

"I felt that surely no one would really throw this away. It was the weirdest thing because I could feel anger coming from this chest. I could feel disbelief; I could feel frustration," Stewart remembers.

Stewart visited the home again with some of the personal pictures, thinking that perhaps the family had been unaware of the false bottom in the reverend's trunk. Again, she checked with the family to make certain they wanted to part with these treasures. She was again assured that she could have whatever had been in the trunks. It seemed to Stewart that the family wanted to get rid of the material. In fact, she thinks that the ghosts may have manifested themselves to the family in a malevolent way and this may account for their desire to trash the trunks—even with the valuable documents and hand-painted silks they contained.

THE SPIRITS MANIFEST FOR STEWART

I think [the spirits manifested themselves] the moment I lifted the bottom of the trunk, and found that hidden compartment, that extra layer. I felt just such a presence," Stewart explains. "I didn't really think about it a whole lot then, but I found myself going through all the documents. I've always admired principles, and admired people who did what they felt was right, and I felt that this is what they were doing. I felt honored to have been able to save them."

Although she senses their presence in her home during the day, Stewart indicates that these spirits usually come to her dreams. Indeed, the spirits had told her in this dream state to get in touch with me, as they have communicated many other messages to Stewart as she slept.

"They started appearing in my dreams. Arnold is much more persistent than Betty is. At first, they would come to me in my dreams as young people—like I had seen them in the photos— because they were thankful that I saved them from going to the dump, and they were thankful that I appreciated their lives.

"As time has progressed and the year has gone by, they have become less pleasant and pushier. Usually when they appear to me in my dreams, if they appear [as their elderly selves] they are not being as nice. They have gotten to where now quite often I don't have to be asleep. They will come and tell me things and do things."

"I am aware of them," Terri continues. "but how do you describe a fragrance? How do you describe an odor? You merely know they are there—it's very subtle."

"Déjà vu" is another way Stewart describes the spirits communications with her, merely Stewart's knowing acknowledgment of what the spirits are telling her. When the spirits get too mischievous, she sometimes has to remind them to back off a bit.

"I have reminded the Johnsons repeatedly because they are very much poltergeists. They are the noisy ghosts; they are very invasive and very persistent. I remind them, that while I am not a Christian, I am the good Samaritan here. I didn't ask to be drawn into this, but in my heart I cannot see someone's life story, especially one so fascinating, go down the drain."

The most frightening moment for Stewart came one evening. She was writing a brief note to herself and as she wrote, she felt the reverend take possession of her hand. She reports that she was both terrified and angry; it felt terribly invasive to have her writing arm "taken over." Furthermore, what she had written in that state turned out to be a reminder from the reverend to contact me and specifically ask if I was a Christian and a Presbyterian. Stewart demanded that the Reverend leave her immediately, and never do such a dreadful thing again.

Stewart reports that she is open to spirits, and that several others live with her in the house on Gordon. She feels that, at some point, several persons had been buried on the property, but she cannot imagine when that may have taken place.

INVESTIGATING THE SPIRITS

While this is one of the most intriguing experiences I've had in writing this book, investigating these spirits has proven to be somewhat frustrating. Of course, neither Stewart nor I would wish to be invasive of the Johnson family, and for this reason, their real name has not been used. After all, it is their right to rid themselves of this collection of dated antiques as they wish, and I did not contact them to investigate this story.

Investigation did reveal that the reverend graduated from Davison College in North Carolina in 1917, and later attended seminary in Virginia. He served as a missionary in China, Japan, and Taiwan, as well as in several interim pastorates in the southeastern United States.

An inscription in one of the booklets from the trunk confirm that the booklet was a gift to Rev. Johnson while he was in Taiwan in 1945. Clearly, the artifacts document the lives of these missionaries in the first half of the twentieth century and therein lies a great deal of history, not to mention the dedication of two missionaries who spent their lives in humble service to their God. Still this is not independent evidence of a haunting or ghostly manifestations.

However, there is the rather strange fact that the spirits brought up my Presbyterian background, and again, Stewart assured me that she did not have than information from the one possible source I could identify, my online vita. She asked this question based on information she obtained from the spirits of the Johnsons.

With that stated, I must state that I am confident that Stewart is sincere in her statements regarding these spirits. She discusses her communication with them as she would a neighbor or a co-worker. In short, I believe her entirely, and perhaps that is where we shall leave this line of inquiry. I can easily believe that someone who spent their entire lives attempting to make a spiritual difference in a distant land would want their efforts remembered. I can only imagine the dissatisfaction of these spirits, as their accomplishments seem to be tossed out to the curb.

AN UNCERTAIN FUTURE

While the spirits of the Johnsons reside still at Stewart's home, she assured me that this is temporary. She has not yet decided what to do with these treasures or the spirits associated with them. Given the historical association with the Amelia Island area, Stewart is considering finding a home for them there. She is certain that these spirits merely want their story told.

AN INTERESTING POSTSCRIPT

In January 2003, I sent an early draft of this story to Stewart for her to review. She sent back a letter suggesting some minor factual changes. As I was traveling when the letter was delivered to my home, my wife, Renet, opened it for me and informed me by phone of Stewart's desired changes. That was all that was said that evening.

The next morning, my wife shared with me a rather unusual dream she had. It involved the two missionaries continually opening and closing the front door to our home, and my wife woke up loudly yelling "Stop it! Stop it!" Stewart has always maintained that these missionaries visit her in dreams, and my wife asked that morning, "Could these guys have hitched a ride in Teri's letter?"

Perhaps we'll never know.

EVIL IN A FOREST PARK BASEMENT

While playing in the fenced backyard one afternoon, young Michelle Trainer wanted a popsicle. She went into the basement space under her family home to retrieve one. As she explains, under the north end of the house, there was a door that opened into a small, unfinished basement where her mother stored homemade popsicles in a deep freeze to which the Michelle and her sisters could help themselves. The basement ran the width of the house, perhaps ten feet, and had an unfinished floor. The basement had only one light, and the back "wall" was merely dirt that rose up to form a normal two-foot crawl space under the remainder of the house. That area was very dark, and it is here that this malevolent spirit appeared.

"It was like cold electricity went through me, and I remember saying 'I'm in terrible danger.' That's the thought I had," Trainer explains today. "I looked into that crawl space in the shadow. Right where it was totally shadowed, I saw two eyes. It sounds like it's out of a movie, I know, but they were two red eyes. . . .

I know what possums look like and I know what dogs look like, and that wasn't this. They were big, red, and it felt like they were glowing."

Little Michelle, while terrified, was not paralyzed by her fear. She slowly backed out of the basement and continued to back her way around the house, without turning her back on the basement or the corner of the house nearest the basement door. She does remember that their large German shepherd—"a great guard dog," as she reports, that was normally very boisterous, loud, and playful—was cowering in the rear of the fenced-in yard, as far from the basement as he could get. When she got in the house, she remembers her mother's reaction was quite unusual.

"I said to her, 'Mom, something evil is in the basement.' She didn't ask me what it was, who, where. I remember her turning the stove off, grabbing the keys and me, and we left."

Apparently her mother knew of strange things happening in the house, since one would normally anticipate that a parent would at least peek into the basement to investigate such a report from her oldest daughter. Michelle was quite young when this happened, and didn't talk with her mother about it at that time. Her mother has since passed away, and Trainer regrets that they never discussed this unusual manifestation.

ONE TRULY MALEVOLENT SPIRIT

It was a quiet street when Michelle Trainer lived on Conley Road in Forest Park. She lived there from the age of two to the age of seven, until 1973. Trainer, who works as a writer and producer with a cable television channel in Atlanta, is now in her thirties. With these experiences as dated as they are, little investigation can be done. Still, Trainer recalls several other times when this vicious spirit appeared.

Once, as she and her younger sister were sleeping in bunk beds in the house, a spirit appeared that her sister described only as a luminous arm and hand, as if a man's arm had been cut off just below the elbow. Her sister woke the entire house with a scream in the middle of the night. Trainer remembers her father rushing in to find nothing other than the young girl screaming hysterically from the top bunk. The girl then described a "bright arm" that had grabbed her arm and had tried to pull her off the top bunk onto the floor. The girl was terrified.

Of course, such an experience would be frightening for a young girl, but most parents would assume that this was just a dream. However, the family took the apparition quite seriously. The young girl's forearm was marked red by what was clearly a handprint and when their father placed his hand next to the grip mark, the print of the fingers were almost half again as large as his own. Clearly, this was not something that the young girl could have done to herself, even if she had clutched her own arm during a dream.

Trainer also recalls the night when, as the family gathered in the living room, they heard something like a shotgun blast from the parents' bedroom. Rushing into the room, everything was in order except for a large oil painting that had fallen to the floor from its normal place over the head of the bed. Surprisingly, the painting had not merely fallen from the wall, it had somehow projected itself across the room and had hit the opposite wall before it crashed to the floor—a trajectory of almost sixteen feet! Trainer's father looked at the opposite wall, then went outside the house with the family in tow to see if something had hit the exterior wall of that bedroom and caused the painting to career across the room so violently. No mark on the exterior wall was found. Also, Trainer recalls that the wire on the back of the painting and the eight-penny nail in the wall itself were both just where they were supposed to be, neither missing or broken. Some unseen hand or spiritual force had tossed this large oil painting across the room.

ANOTHER GHOST, THIS ONE BENIGN?

While all of the experiences above were "evil" in Trainer's view, she does recall another manifestation in this house that was not. This may suggest a different spirit in addition to the one described above. When they reached a certain age, the sisters' bunk beds were separated and were used as twin beds by the girls. Michelle remembers awakening one evening and seeing a man with a rounded, enlarged head looking at her from above her bed. She remembers that she could see through him, and that he looked somehow "bluish." She remembers thinking that the guy looked like Frankenstein, and that she wasn't afraid of Frankenstein. She didn't feel danger from this spirit; nothing like her terror when she saw the glowing eyes in the basement. So, rather than screaming, she merely looked at this ghostly image for a time "in a staring contest," as she called it, until it vanished as silently as it had come.

The next day, Trainer recalls one of her young friends mentioning the car accident that had happened in her front yard the night before. The house was on a curve, and many drivers would drive very fast down the street in front of the house. Several times while Trainer lived there, car accidents occurred resulting in wrecked cars literately in the family's front yard! On the night when Trainer had seen the spirit, a motorcycle accident had taken place on the Conley Road curve and Michelle's mother—a nurse—had tried desperately, though unsuccessfully, to revive the injured cyclist in their front yard. He died there on the same night little Michelle had seen the bluish spirit with the rounded, enlarged head.

Trainer doesn't recall if she ever shared this experience with her parents or her sister; indeed there were many other evil hauntings to deal with in this house, and this particular manifestation seemed fairly benign. Further, Trainer assumes that her mother had chosen not to tell her young daughters of the gory death in their front yard the night before, since they were frightened enough in this house. However, Trainer believes to this day that the apparition's rounded, enlarged head was actually the 1970s-style motorcycle helmet that the motorcyclist had been wearing.

NO INVESTIGATION OPTIONS

There is no way to further investigate this story, as Trainer discussed during our interview. Further, since both her mother and her sister have passed away; we are left with only one eye witness to these chilling events from over thirty years ago.

Trainer does report that she has lived in another house that had a resident spirit, but that most of the places she has lived have not. This suggests something positive about her credibility, and her testimony is completely believable. Michelle has taken these manifestations very seriously. She is a member of a group that hunts for evidence of spirits in Georgia and elsewhere, the Ghost Hounds.

HER FATHER'S VISITS IN LAKE CLAIRE

Do spirits offer emotional support to those they leave behind in death? Can ghosts offer comfort to the living? In the death of a loved one, many emotions come into play, and it is often difficult to separate one's emotional reactions—perhaps even one's emotional needs—from true hauntings. Still, those of us seeking spirits must trust the words, the emotions, and the impressions of those who have experienced manifestations, and who can say what a "true haunting" really is.

Susan Beeching lives on Connecticut Avenue in a stylish old home in the Lake Claire area of Atlanta with her husband of twenty-one years and their two children. She also believes that spirit of her deceased father resides with them. While she has not seen her father in the house she believes that she has sensed his presence a number of times since his death.

Hr father and mother were divorced many years ago, and he lived in Hertford, Connecticut. (Note the interesting fact that he lived in Connecticut, and Beeching lives on Connecticut Avenue). Her father did have roots in Georgia, having grown up in Eatonton, Georgia, and being schooled in Atlanta early in his life. He'd lived in Hartford for a number of years, having met Beeching's mother at Yale, and subsequently remaining in the state.

Even after her parents' divorce, Beeching remained very close to him; she enjoyed his sense of humor and his zest for life. During his last days, she was visiting him and realized that his death was near. He died late one evening, and she called her brother to inform him of his passing.

The next morning, her brother and sister-in-law were driving over to the house in Hartford where she was staying, to get her and take her to the hospital to attend to the necessary paperwork. Beeching was crammed in the middle of the small truck her brother drove, and was not generally looking out of the window. However, at one point something told her to look up, and when she did she immediately saw the name "Wallace"—her father's first name—written on a sign. She sensed his presence immediately.

"I just knew it was him, telling me he was o.k. I just knew it was him," she explains. "Later I drove by the sign again, and saw that it said 'Wallace Painting and Contracting' but when I saw it that first time, it was like something told me to look at that sign, and all I'd seen was one word—his name."

Of course, this emotional reaction to the sign could suggest that Beeching was struggling with the death of a loved one, rather than experiencing a true haunting. Still, the unusual situations had only begun.

Beeching continued her tale of unusual circumstances by telling of a shopping trip a week after she buried her father. There she ran into a woman she worked with who had become a great friend and, in some sense, a counselor for Beeching during her father's long illness.

"The first weekend I was back in Atlanta, around November 10, I was in a grocery store, shopping." Beeching remembers. "A lady that I worked with was there, and she doesn't live anywhere near that store; there's no reason for her to be over there shopping. It is really strange that she was there. She is a very spiritual person, and while I'm not a religious person, she had helped me when I was very sad over my dad's sickness, she had helped me tremendously. She said that she was driving by and not really intending to go shopping but that something told her to go to that store. She said that she just felt like she had to stop there. I knew my dad had sent her, even though he'd never met her. He'd sent her to help me get through my sadness."

About a month after her father's death, she was sorting through old Christmas cards and, as she always does, she was recycling them by cutting out attractive pictures for use as place cards or name tags for presents. She works quickly, never even bothering to read the signatures on the cards.

"One card seemed to come into my hand, as if it was meant to. And it was a card from my dad. Of course, I had to read that card, and it said: 'Hey, kiddo! I'm thinking about you! Hang in there!' That is something that my dad would have said, and I knew he was out there, keeping an eye on me."

Beeching also tells of several dreams she'd had of him. One dream in particular seems to defy logic. In it she saw her parents and herself sitting together in a restaurant. One can only wonder why that particular restaurant was critical to her dream, but Beeching was insistent that it was a certain chain restaurant. Also, her parents had been divorced for over twenty years at that point; why would she see them together in this dream? During the dream, she realized that while she could see her father, the waiter and her mother could not. She remembers telling him that she was having a "huge problem" because she was talking to him while the waiter and her mother couldn't see him. They might think she was crazy.

At a later point in the dream, Beeching told her father that she needed to know that he was alright. He indicated that he was fine, but that he didn't realize that she had this intense need to hear from him.

EVIDENCE FOR THIS SPIRIT

I hesitate to write this story for several reasons. First of all, it is quite a personal story, involving a very close love between a daughter and her father; aside from an example of family love, I'm not sure this story is anyone else's business. Further, this story doesn't present any of the usual indicators of a true haunting. There is no single spiritual manifestation here that seems supernatural. Finally, there is only one witness to this spirit, if this is a spirit.

When I asked if Beeching believed in spirits, she indicated that she believed that persons after death could let their families know that they are o.k. Beeching indicated that she doesn't believe in the Hollywood stereotype of ghosts (a glowing white entity) and really is not sure about poltergeists at all, but that she does think that family members could make their presence known.

Of course, there are no levitating objects or sightings of spirits in the hallways in Beeching's story, so there seem to be few ways to further investigate this haunting. Still, Beeching is entirely believable. She's a banker by profession and a loving, caring mother. Further, she had no reason at all to share this story, other than a desire to get these experiences on record in some way and to document these occurrences. Still, she is adamant that her father has made his presence felt in her life since his death.

This story does represent many other stories in which persons in emotionally tense times believe that they are comforted by spirits. As such, I offer this example of a unsubstantiated haunting that really can't be investigated further. It does suggest that what we often interpret as our personal emotional efforts to work through the death of a loved one really may be spiritual interventions to help us along. It would be comforting to believe that our deceased loved ones are there for us—perhaps they are.

FACES IN THE WINDOWS

SPIRITS OF THE WINECOFF HOTEL FIRE

In the mysterious twilight that passes for night amid the downtown city lights, the old hotel stands still, nestled in the corner of Ellis and Peachtree streets among the sights and sounds that create the very image of downtown Atlanta. Residents, businesspeople, and tourists pass this building everyday, unaware of its dark, deadly history or the mysteries hidden in its deserted rooms and hallways. Only by looking up into the broken windows on the upper floors does one get the sense, only an impression really, that those permanently darkened windows are somehow alive. Those gloomy holes of this supposedly "fireproof" hotel seem responsive to one's gaze; one can almost see the nameless faces of the hundred-plus souls, tortured and damned, who burned alive there or jumped to their death on Peachtree Street.

On December 7, 1946, the first photographer on the scene, Georgia Institute of Technology student Arnold Hardy, took a picture of those doomed faces in the windows, the faces of hotel guests on the higher-floors—pleading,

As you walk past late in the evening, gaze up at the windows of the old Winecoff Hotel at Peachtree and Ellis streets, and don't be surprised to see the faces of some of the tortured spirits, damned by the flames of long ago, looking back.

hopeless faces. Hardy also took the now-infamous picture of forty-one-year-old Daisy McCumber, captured midair; as she jumped eleven stories from the certain death above—and managed to survive the fall. Hardy won a Pulitzer Prize for that photo—the only amateur photographer to ever win that coveted award. Today, the building is vacant, save the spirits who died a horrible death there, some burning alive, some dying from smoke inhalation, some simply jumping to their deaths on Peachtree Street. Their faces are in the windows, rarely seen, but felt by many.

Long before Atlanta assumed its skyline of today, when fifteen-story buildings were the tallest around, the Winecoff Hotel dominated this part of the city. It was built in 1913 and was for a time the tallest building around. Once heralded as "Atlanta's Finest Hotel," the Winecoff was the hotel of choice for the decades spanning World War I and World War II.

The Winecoff stands today only as an empty shell of a building, occupied only by the homeless, the unfortunates who occasionally break in the windows on the first floor and help themselves to the free living space of a hundred and fifty hotel rooms. The local police round these people up every so often and hear the tales of strange events—weird images of half-seen people or the ones who disappear in an instant. Of course, these stories coming from the homeless don't result in much investigation—after all, what haven't some of these vagabonds seen in their altered states of drug-induced terror?

THE DEADLY FIRE

The Winecoff Hotel was filled to capacity with holiday shoppers, soldiers who were being discharged from the hard-fought war that defined the twentieth century, and teenagers from all over Georgia who were in the big city for a mock legislative session. Some permanent or semi-permanent residents also made their home in this plush establishment so near the center of this vibrant city. On that night, there were 279 souls in the building and 160 thankfully escaped with their lives.

Perhaps a cigarette was dropped by a late-night partygoer—although some suspect arson—but around 3:40 A. M. on December 7, 1946, a fire broke out and quickly crept up the central staircases. In that age, no fire doors protected the individual hallways, no sprinkler systems were in place, and no outside fire escapes were required. While construction codes had been strengthened in 1943 (as a result of several major hotel fires in the United States and the knowledge gained when much of London was burned in the Blitz), the 1913 Winecoff was grandfathered into the law underwent no renovations. The Winecoff billed itself as fireproof on the grounds of its largely brick construction.

Of course, the wooden frame inside the old building provided tinder for the sweeping fire. The central staircase served as an excellent chimney for fanning the blaze through doorless hallways. With such fuel and a readily available air supply, the structure was largely ablaze in under twenty minutes.

One hundred and nineteen lives were lost, most of them above the level of the fire ladders mounted on trucks outside. Arnold Hardy saw only two nets to capture those jumping from the higher windows—he recalled wondering why every fire engine was not provided with a jump net. Many saved themselves by scrambling down ropes hastily made from bedsheets. Wooden beams or shorter fire ladders were placed between windows in the Winecoff and the roof of the Carnegie Building next door; these served as planks on which many escaped.

For over two and a half hours, fire companies from all over northern Georgia fought the raging blaze, even as many hotel guests gave up hope and jumped to their deaths. We can only imagine the frustration of the firemen as they witnessed these jumps, a phenomenon which has become all too terribly etched in our recent past during the destruction of the World Trade Center in 2001.

By the early morning of December 7, the fire was over, as were the lives of 119 men, women, and children. It was, for many years, the worst hotel fire in history. The victims included William Fleming Winecoff, the hotel's builder and a resident of one of the tenth-floor suites, and his wife Grace. Perhaps their faces are among those sometimes seen in the hotel's blackened windows, perhaps they occasionally visit their home and terrify the homeless inhabiting the building.

UNEASY FEELINGS

We are left with few ways to investigate these specters. With so much tragic death, it would be a wonder if there were not strange occurrences at this once stately downtown landmark. Still, take the time to look up into the darkened windows, speculate, and perhaps catch a glimpse of the scared faces from that terrible night.

THE WREN'S NEST

THE SPIRIT FROM UNCLE REMUS

The ghost at the Wren's Nest, home of author Joel Chandler Harris, is never threatening, is never intimidating; rather, this young spirit seems somewhat tentative toward, even frightened of the few who have seen him. The small child, about seven years old, appears only rarely today in the dark recesses of the front foyer and stairway. As one may expect, this spirit is surrounded by world-famous characters from his father's Uncle Remus folktales including Brer Rabbit and Brer Fox. Ghost hunter Nancy Roberts surmised that this was the spirit of Linton Harris, Harris's young son who lived here at the Wren's Nest and died at the age of seven.

This portion of the cottage was not original to the 1870 frame house constructed by George Muse (founder of Atlanta's Muse's Clothing Store), but the male children who originally had been sleeping in the downstairs hallway were moved after an 1884 remodeling into a steeply gabled upper-floor room with several nine-over-nine windows facing the road. The reluctant spirit wears turn-

Linton Harris, circa 1885. *Special Collections, Robert W. Woodruff Library, Emory University.*

of-the-century clothes and is usually seen when the lights are dim.

One would expect to find spirits aplenty intertwined in the folklore that surrounds this Queen Anne-style landmark on Ralph David Abernathy Drive in southwest Atlanta. The story of a famous author, suffering through the death of his son when the child was only seven, is a tale that is appropriately sad, just right for giving rise to spirits. One would be almost surprised *not* to find ghosts here.

The cottage is itself quite unusual, a rambling collection of large, high-ceilinged rooms that are collected around a series of entryways and hallways running down the center. Perhaps due to the fact that it was built in several stages, the asymmet-

Does this famous old cottage on the National Register of Historic Places house the spirit of a young boy? The five upstairs windows mark the sleeping quarters for the male children, including Linton Harris. *LOC*

rical house seems to go on forever. The front portion of the house features, quite prominently, a central foyer and a three-run staircase so tall and narrow it seems to wind to the heavens. This is where the ghost of a small boy is said to visit, perhaps on his way to the sleeping quarters that were originally meant to serve as his father's study and writing room. While Harris had several male children who died before maturity—he referred to all his children as "dearest chums and partners"— Linton seems to be of the appropriate age, having died in 1890 when he was only seven years old.

The front foyer and staircase of the Wren's Nest is the center the house's ghostly occurrences. *LOC*

Linton is buried at Westview Cemetery only a few miles distant, near the grave of his father. His small grave is identified by an unremarkable stone that would not otherwise suggest a restless spirit.

THE BIRTH OF UNCLE REMUS

Having a famous parent is never easy on a young man, but Linton passed away while only seven, and one may well wonder about his understanding of his father's fame at such a tender age. Of course, he would have understood that his father was a writer, since Joel Chandler Harris was then writing for the *Atlanta Constitution*. Also, he must have heard the wonderful stories of Brer Rabbit, Brer Fox, Brer B'ar, and Jack Sparrow at his father's knee, a genuine treasure for a young boy of any age. Harris also wrote "genuine myth-stories," tales about ha'nts, boogers, "cunjer folks," "Jacky-my-lanterns," and even Ole Scratch himself. The tales were told and written on the house's heavily latticed front porch. Linton, the Harrises' fifth son, was particularly enamored of his father's tales and would listen to these stories for hours.

Harris, by all accounts, was a loving father and the Harrises' was a happy home filled with love and laughter, which comes as a surprise since he was himself was something of a social outcast as a child. His father disappeared shortly after his birth and in that day and age in his small Georgia birthplace of Eatonton, polite society did not socialize with such women or their children. This absence of a male role model in his early life probably assured that Harris would explore elsewhere, opening himself to other cultural influences. Indeed, he often visited neighboring slave cabins in the evening to sit at the feet of several wonderful storytellers, another experience which polite society would have frowned upon!

Harris worked as a young man at the Turnwold Plantation near Augusta, Georgia, where over a hundred slaves were then laboring. He was on the plantation from the early 1860s until approximately 1866, witnessing the destruction of the old slave economy that provided so much of the labor to build the Old South.

Author Joel Chandler Harris originally called his southwest Atlanta home Snap Bean Farm, but renamed it the Wren's Nest after a small wren took up residence in his mailbox. *Frances Benjamin Johnston, LOC*

In slave populations of the size at Turnwold Plantation, there were always several storytellers around, sharing remnants of the rich African folktales that had been altered for the slave culture of the day. Strong African influences could be heard in these wonderful old tales, and as a young man of thirteen, Harris must have sat mesmerized at the feet of these worldly wise slaves by the cabin fires. While "Uncle Remus" himself never existed, his persona represents an amalgam of several storytellers from the Turnwold Plantation including two known today only as Uncle George Terrel and Aunt Sissy. Many years later,

Harris's Uncle Remus stories brought a rich cultural tradition of storytelling to life, first in a small newspaper column called "Uncle Remus Animal Stories" and later in collections of the various tales.

Here rests the body of a small boy. Linton Harris spirit frolics playfully in the downstairs foyer and the upstairs sleeping quarters of the Wren's Nest.

These stories, considered politically incorrect in the 1970s and 1980s because of their many unflattering stereotypes of African Americans, have seen a resurgence in popularity today. Profound wisdom and biting humor of the African folktale can be seen even in Harris' embellished and biased retellings; these African-influenced stories provide moral guidance and deep insight into human character.

Because of the popularity and worldwide recognition of these tales during Harris's life, Harris himself became one of the most prominent Atlanta citizens during his later years. Many folks in Atlanta would walk by the house merely to see if they could catch a glimpse of the famous author, who in later years did much of his writing on the front porch of the house.

LITTLE EVIDENCE HERE

I visited the Wren's Nest one winter morning, and was treated to a wonderful tour of the old home. The characters from the Uncle Remus tales come to life in the short video on the life and influences of Joel Chandler Harris. Further, stuffed life-sized characters from the stories are on display in the hallway—Brer Rabbit, Brer Fox, and Brer B'ar all are here, standing together as if to challenge the beliefs of each visitor to the home.

After the tour, I explained my work on this book, and noted the reports of a young boy haunting the front hallway. I asked the guide that day about her experiences with the ghost. Unfortunately, she indicated that she'd had no such experiences and did not know of anyone who had. This left very few follow-up possibilities for me on this famous Atlanta haunting. The guide did, however, indicate that while the house itself was open to the public, the upstairs room where the male children slept was not open, nor were the several basement "kitchens and store rooms." She said the basement rooms were particularly scary; she thought there were "critters" down there in the several basements, and that she wouldn't go down there for any reason. Presumably she meant spiders and snakes, but one has to wonder what troubled young spirits could wander in those dark recesses of these basements, visiting in the cool evenings the upper stairway and front foyer of this old house.

THE BLUE LADY AND OTHER SPIRITS OF
AGNES SCOTT COLLEGE

The Blue Lady is occasionally seen in the upper windows of Presser Hall on the campus of Agnes Scott College in Decatur, Georgia; she appears as a bluish light, warning all who care to hear of blood and battles now distant in time. The light is the spirit of a woman who seeks forever to fulfill her appointed task, that of raising the alarm of the advance on Atlanta of General William Tecumseh Sherman's Union Army during the bleak days of July 1864.

As the story goes, a church was once located on this hill, on the west end of the current college campus, one of the highest points of land on the Agnes Scott campus. In those days, churches were frequently located on hilltops, and in that pre-skyscraper-era church steeples were often the highest point around. The church was located no more than five hundred yards from downtown Decatur. Thus, for a host of geographical and practical reasons, this would have been a perfect location to raise the alarm that Sherman's powerful Union army of some hundred thousand troops were digging in around the city defenses of Atlanta, about two miles away. This lady—no one seems to have recorded her name—was given the task of raising the alarm.

However, the ghostly stories all suggest that she was killed before she could raise her warning to the distant Confederates. Failing in that task, and seeing the subsequent destruction of the Confederacy, this spirit wanders today in the structure that has replaced the old church, Presser Hall. Some say the Blue Lady

The Blue Lady is sometimes seen in the upper windows of Agnes Scott's Presser Hall, late in the evening, warning of the pending doom of the Confederacy as Sherman's army of yesteryear approaches.

is seen as a shifting bluish light in that building's gothic-influenced music center and chapel, whereas others say only a light is seen.

A few college publications mention the numerous ghostly tales associated with the campus, as well as one version of this story. In that version, the ghostly lady is a widow, who roams the grounds today searching for her husband who died in the battle.

Another spiritual manifestation involves rumors of sightings and a "feeling of uneasiness" that some students have reported in Dana Fine Arts Building on campus. A female art professor, whose name has been lost, was killed in an accident in that building in the 1960s. The accident involved a machine used in making and coloring pottery, but details were sketchy. Through the years, many students report being uneasy in the fine arts building, particularly when working on their art projects late into the night; indeed, some students refuse to work in that building alone in the evening.

Yet another Agnes Scott spirit is a trustee who fought against the idea of installing an elevator in Presser Hall. It is said her spirit haunts the elevator that was eventually installed; it will often move to various floor, even when no one has punched any buttons.

HISTORY BEHIND THE TALE

It is true that the Battle of Atlanta involved some fighting on a portion of the Agnes Scott campus. One historic marker commemorating those distant days of the Civil War sits on the northwest corner of the grounds. It was placed in 1921 and marks the left end of the Union line of earthworks, a defensive point that was attacked during the Battle of Atlanta in July 1864. Also, history records that various cavalry actions took place in downtown Decatur only a few blocks away. These events are marked with numerous historical markers near the DeKalb County Courthouse in downtown Decatur, some eight blocks distant.

During the Battle of Atlanta, General John B. Hood's Confederate forces left the defensive works around Atlanta on several occasions to attack the Union army under Sherman. In fact, the left end of Sherman's line was the point at which Hood had planned a bold flanking strike. During the night of July 21, 1864, Hood withdrew Major-General Benjamin F. Cheatham's troops from the outer Confederate defensive works around Atlanta to the inner works closer to downtown in an effort to mislead Sherman. The abandoned line of

Confederate Atlanta was defended in the Battle of Atlanta by a perimeter of palisades and chevaux-de-frise designed by Lemuel P. Grant, namesake of the city's Grant Park. *George N. Barnard, 1864, LOC*

Confederate breastworks stretched some three miles astride the Georgia Railroad, crossing the tracks approximately where the present-day Reynold-stown MARTA station stands.

At the same time, Hood reassigned Major-General's William J. Hardee's men to hike fifteen miles to the south to get behind Sherman's hastily constructed line—the left end of which was on land today part of the Agnes Scott campus—and "hook" to the north to roll up the southern end of the Union line. This was to be coordinated with an attack by Cheatham's Corps along the four-mile Union front, as well as a cavalry action in nearby Decatur.

While Sherman was taken in by the ruse, believing Atlanta to have been abandoned during the night of July 21, Major-General James B. McPherson, whose troops were on the left flank of the Union line, was worried about his exposed southern flank. Sherman had sent all of his cavalry—the eyes and ears of every army in those days—off to destroy railroads in central Georgia. McPherson sent a corps under General Granville Dodge to guard the Union's southern flank, and thus inadvertently put them directly astride the planned attack point for Hardee's Confederate troops. This made for a very bloody battle.

The attack along the line came on the afternoon of July 22, 1864. Confederates recaptured their original line for a time at the now-famous Railroad Cut (under the current Reynoldstown MARTA station), but lost it again in fairly short order. Attacks by Hardee's Corps were scattered through the area from Decatur back towards the southwest. The fighting everywhere was bloody, fearsome, and determined. History records that the Confederates came within an inch of a great victory. However, because of the relocation of Dodge's Union Corps, the Union prevailed. Leave it said that the ground of Decatur—and more pointedly of Agnes Scott College—was drenched with much blood—Confederate and Union—on that fateful day.

RUMORS OF THE SPIRITS AT AGNES SCOTT

While rumors abound of the Blue Lady, those I interviewed on campus could not locate anyone who had actually seen this apparition; still the story persists through generation of students. More pointedly, no one could be found who had directly seen any of these manifestations. Thus, the reader is again left with tales of spirits, and little evidence. Are these just the musings of young women seeking their education at one of the preeminent women's colleges in the South? Or do spirits abound at Agnes Scott?

SMITTY'S ASHES IN MORNINGSIDE

The spirit on North View Drive in the Morningside neighborhood of Atlanta was the first spirit encountered by the Casey family. One night, when Emily Casey was very young, the loud crash awoke her entire family. Casey remembers this as if it were yesterday, since she and her younger sister were asleep in the bedroom where the crash occurred. Their parents found the contents of the three shelves attached to the wall opposite the girls' bed had been swiped to the ground, as if in one motion some unseen presence had run its hand along every shelf, pushing everything to a broken heap on the floor. This mischief-making spirit had announced itself with a flourish.

The Caseys heard from the spirit several other times. Both sisters report that on many evenings they heard footsteps in the hallway near the picture frame when no one was physically there. The girls' mother felt that some type of "presence" had entered the house ever since she and her husband had obtained an old picture frame from a supposedly haunted house in Michigan. Mrs. Casey decided to use the frame for her own wedding picture, and didn't really believe that the object was haunted at first. Still, as events like those noted above increased in frequency, Mrs. Casey and her daughters all began to accept that a spirit had invaded their home. They were somewhat relieved when their father decided to purchase a duplex next door, and move the family into that home. Little did they realize that they would be trading in one spirit for two.

SMITTY'S ASHES

The Smiths lived in a duplex on North View Avenue. Neither of the Casey girls knew Mr. Smith in life, but they recall very well his antics after death. The duplex was built in 1927, and the girls were told during their childhood that Mr. Smith had passed away in 1947. His wife survived until 1981, at which time the Caseys purchased the property and moved into one half of the duplex.

When the family bought the building and began to clean it out, they were surprised to find that all of the Smiths' furniture was left in the house. Indeed, they found all of Mr. Smith's personal effects, such as his clothes, razor, even still-refrigerated bottles of his medicine that had expired thirty-four years previous. These items had been left just as they had been at his death in 1947! It was almost as if Mrs. Smith had preserved the left side of the duplex as some type of memorial to her late husband; she'd never rented out either side of the house. Of course, all this would have been strange enough, but when they found the ashes of Mr. Smith sitting in an urn on the mantel, they realized they were dealing with something quite unusual.

Mr. Casey located Mrs. Smith in a close-by nursing home and took the small urn containing her husband's ashes to her, thinking that it had been a mistake on her part—the forgetfulness of an older lady—to leave the urn behind. He reported to his daughter, many years later, that when he tried to return the ashes to Mrs. Smith she—quite literally—freaked out in the nursing home, shouting at him to leave her alone and to take the ashes away with him! Given this obvious lack of concern for the ashes on the widow's part, the Caseys decided that they would keep them out of respect for the dead; they lovingly nicknamed them "Smitty." They didn't realize at the time that they were keeping another spirit!

Smitty's ashes were found on the mantel in the left side of this housee on North View Avenue. Does his spirit still stalk the unwary residents late at night?

Mrs. Casey was the first to notice that, as the family began to clean and paint the new duplex, the ashes would apparently move themselves. The presence of the ashes disturbed her, so while she was working on that side of the duplex, she would move the urn to a spot over the mantel in the right-hand side of the house. Nevertheless, the next morning, Smitty's urn would be sitting proudly in its accustomed spot above the left-side mantel! The family noted this ghostly movement of Smitty on a number of occasions.

Over time, Smitty has made himself known in other ways as well. As recently as 1998, after college, marriage, and beginning her own family, Casey and her husband had occasion to rent the left side of the duplex for a period of six months from Casey's mother. The building has been in the family since 1981, and Casey understood that Smitty was a rather benign spirit. She really didn't mind living in the house, and while the ashes themselves had long ago been disposed of, the "presence" is still in the house.

Casey reports that her compact disc player often "self-select" songs, in the middle of other musical selections. When doors often open by themselves, family members merely say, "Hi, Smitty!" and go on about their business.

UNRELATED SPIRITS AND
UNANSWERED QUESTIONS

As something of a skeptic, I was somewhat concerned with this story, even though I did have two witnesses reporting on these events. The two spirits who have taken up residence in houses that are side by side bring up a couple of questions. It was apparent that both Casey sisters were reasonably serious young women: one a mother of two small children and the other a young professional working in a large media production company in Atlanta. Each was a very credible witness.

I began to wonder if these women were particularly sensitive to spirits, so I asked both sisters if they found spirits in every house in which they lived. Each reported that, while they believe in "something," they had lived in a number of places that were not haunted, as well as a few places that were. The fact that Mrs. Smith kept a "museum" dedicated to her husband may suggest that some spirit had made itself known to her—she did react violently when she had the option of taking the ashes in the nursing home; clearly she wanted nothing to do with Mr. Smith's belongings or his ashes when she finally moved away from North View Avenue. Unfortunately, she has since passed away and was not available for an interview relative to these spirits.

Again, we are left with witnesses to some unexplained spiritual manifestations but with little real history that can be explored. Again, the frustration associated with rumors of spirits sets in.

IV

GHOSTS OF ATHENS AND NORTH GEORGIA

Atlanta is a new city, having been formed as a specifically selected rail-transportation hub in 1836. By that date, its sister city, Athens, Georgia, was already a settled community. Athens was settled well before 1800 and was officially incorporated in 1806. The Classic City had been chosen as the home of the University of Georgia, the state's flagship public institution of higher learning, in 1785. The campus has been the seedbed for Georgia leaders for more than two hundred years, thus creating a symbiotic relationship between these two cities: Athens educates attorneys at the UGA law school, and Atlanta employs them in the state legislature.

In seeking ghosts that predate Atlanta's brief history, it seemed reasonable to investigate the spectral depth of the Atlanta/Athens relationship. The distance between the two cities—only seventy-five miles—is no distance at all to a ghost. With this brief introduction, following is a survey of spirits in and around Athens and northeast Georgia.

CAPTAIN PEELER'S FIRE HALL

In 1995, Athens built a civic center complex, the Classic Center, that since has hosted performances by some of the best theater and music groups in the world. Concerts, drama, opera, and ballet, as well as meetings and conventions, are housed in this modern facility. The center houses a theater, auditoriums, meeting rooms, and administrative offices—as well as a resident ghost.

Finding an appropriate downtown location for the sprawling complex was something of a difficulty, and, while a few locations were discussed, the planners settled on a location off Thomas Street in the 1990s. While few would miss the warehouses which were to be torn down to make room for the complex, the historic Fire Hall No. 1. sat almost dead center in the middle of the several properties.

After much controversy, the Athens-Clarke County government showed excellent judgment by hiring architects Rabun-Hatch to incorporate the historic firehouse into the design of the complex. The old fire hall was in use as a fire station until 1989, and then served as the offices of the local chamber of

In Athens's former Fire Hall No. 1, the spirit of Captain H. Peeler still roams. His ghostly image has been spotted in the glass of the front double doors—the doors once used by old horse-drawn pump wagons and early motorized fire trucks.

commerce. The firehouse was reconfigured to include a small auditorium downstairs, administrative offices upstairs, and a basement. The massive firehouse doors were cut through to retrofit two ticket windows. One can almost hear the fire alarms and see the horse-drawn pump trucks tear from this old hall to battle the numerous city fires in that distant era. Clearly, the preservation of this historic treasure has been a boon to downtown Athens and also has given the city one of its best ghost stories.

SPOTTING CAPTAIN PEELER'S GHOST

Having read published accounts of a ghost in the fire hall, I visited the building. I asked the young woman at the information desk the innocuous, yet engaging question, "Do you folks happen to have a ghost I can borrow?" Without batting an eye, the receptionist answered, "You will need to speak to Ms. Wolfe, our administrator."

Of course, at that moment, I assumed that this young woman didn't share—or even understand—my sense of humor in formulating that question so carefully. I even thought that she might well wish me ill-will, because my query was not one of the more mundane and typical questions asked of an information-booth employee (e.g. "Where's the john?"). In short, I assumed that I would be quickly brushed off by the administrator upstairs.

Once upstairs, I asked the same question to Kathy Wolfe, the center's director of administrative services for the classic center, and you can only imagine my surprise when she responded, "Oh. You mean Captain Peeler. I've seen him myself." I was then greeted with the biggest smile I have ever seen, along with a welcoming handshake.

Wolfe told the story of returning to work after lunch one afternoon, she approached the building in full view of the ticket windows and glass doors retrofitted behind the original, large wooden doors which are kept open during business hours. While Wolfe waiting at a crosswalk approximately thirty-five yards from the fire hall, she noticed someone looking out the doors on the left. She reports that he was wearing a uniform, and while his face was not clear, the uniform was dark and looked somewhat old. She knew that none of the center's employees had been issued that type of uniform.

She continues: "When I got into the building, there was no one in the room, no one in the fire hall at all, and there was not enough time . . . by the time I got into the building, for someone to just leave."

The lower floor of the fire hall, immediately behind the entrance doors, is a 2,800 square foot open space, which originally housed fire wagons, and now serves as a meeting and party space. Thus, someone would have had to walk a considerable distance to hide around a corner by the time Wolfe entered the doors. Once she got into the building and found no one, she felt a rather strange sensation: "Oh, I just . . . I think I just saw Capt. Peeler!"

She knew of Capt. Peeler from former center employees who had some rather strange experiences. She'd also heard stories of noises on the steps when no one was in the building from some of the firefighters who had formerly worked there in the 1980s and before.

Seeing Capt. Peeler didn't make her uncomfortable. "No. Not at all!" she says. "He just does what he does." In fact, in all accounts of Capt. Peeler's antics, there has never been any reason for fright or nervousness. Retired firefighters have visited the old fire hall and related stories of hearing Capt. Peeler walking up and down the stairs, but there has never been an example of malicious intent by the captain.

UNUSUAL MANIFESTATIONS

Wolfe is not the only recent employee who has experienced strange things in this building. Another female employee was working late one evening to finish some paperwork and walked into the kitchen area to get a drink of water. She noticed that several drawers were pulled partially open, and thinking nothing of it at the time, she simply closed them. However, as she left the room, she heard the rather unusual squeak of wood on wood and turned back towards the drawers. They were opened again. At that point, this employee decided to leave the building and let the work wait until co-workers could join her in the old fire hall the next morning.

According to numerous accounts, ghosts can and frequently do manifest themselves by toying with physical objects, and these opening drawers may represent Capt. Peeler's way of saying, "I'm here!"

Further, Capt. Peeler apparently manifests himself in such a way that makes the numerous security cameras flicker in unexpected ways. Classic Center Director of Security Randy Eaton oversees the seven or eight security cameras in the system. The cameras randomly feed into one central viewing monitor. However, at certain times, the system seems to shift to an unexpected camera in such an unusual way (i.e., in a way that would be impossible given the system's programming), that some of the security officers thought the system may be detecting some movement. However, to date, no specifically ghostly images had appeared.

THE SPIRIT OF CAPTAIN PEELER?

Unlike the identity of certain other Athens specters, this ghost's is fairly unambiguous. By all accounts, this particular apparition is the ghost of an Athens fireman from some seventy-five years ago. Hiram H. Peeler was born in 1861 and ended his distinguished career as a captain in the Athens Fire Department upon his death in 1928. He had served as a firefighter for forty-seven of his sixty-seven years. He began his career in 1881, meaning he would have used both horse-drawn and motorized firefighting equipment. It behooves us to contemplate the dramatic changes in firefighting technology in Capt. Peeler's world.

For his first twenty years or so, he would have worked in a world where fireplaces and wood- and coal-burning stoves were the primary means of heating and cooking, and where city waterworks were not yet envisioned. Needless to say, such heat sources could and did create a large number of fires in homes and businesses. A gas works company had been formed in Athens in 1852, only nine years before Peeler's birth, and the lamps it made possible were by many accounts unreliable and thus added yet another cause for frequent fires in the downtown area. Further, the lack of citywide waterworks and the spottiness of downtown's system of underground cisterns for firefighting meant that Capt. Peeler's Fire Company No. 1 had to haul water to fires much more frequently than do modern firefighters. The horse-drawn water wagons and cisterns would have represented the entire firefighting infrastructure available to Capt. Peeler's company.

By the end of Capt. Peeler's career in the late 1920s, electricity provided most of the city's lighting, safe and reliable gas stoves for cooking were in common use, and furnaces, rather than fireplaces, were the norm. Citywide waterworks and fast-moving fire engines were used. The world seemed to be moving forward at a hectic pace.

CAPTAIN PEELER PREFERS THE OLDER EQUIPMENT

Inside the Classic Center—and sometimes displayed within the old fire hall itself—is an antique horse-drawn fire wagon, which served as the fire chief's carriage. This particular fire wagon saw service during the years that Captain Peeler would have been fighting fires in Athens, during the later part of the 1800s. Some experiences of Capt. Peeler suggest that he is attracted to this relic from a bygone age.

Director of Security Eaton who often works in the old fire hall, had an eerie experience with Capt. Peeler's specter. Eaton responsibilities include managing a security team of ten to safeguard all Classic

Is Captain Hiram H. Peeler's spirit attracted to his old fire chief's wagon? He was spotted standing near this wagon by an employee of Athens's convention center—then just as quickly disappeared.

Center property, furniture, and historical relics, such as the old fire wagon.

One evening in 1998, Eaton released his set-up crew around midnight, after they had finished preparing for a conference coming into the complex the next morning. He had directed the security team to secure the building and that task had been completed. Eaton then got on the elevator in the new section of the Classic Center building and exited on the first floor, near where the old fire chief's wagon was on display. He glanced through an open double door to his left as he was turning to the right down the hall, and he noticed an older gentleman in some type of dark uniform standing next to the wagon. Eaton turned right and continued on his way down the hallway "only for a moment" before he remembered that there should not be anyone in the display area at all, at that time of night, and with the security procedures already completed. He turned around and looked straight back down the hall towards the man, but saw only the old wagon.

According to Eaton, it took "only a second" to turn away and then turn back towards the wagon, and the figure of the man was gone in that flickering of time. It was only then that Eaton thought that he might just have seen the ghost of Capt. Peeler.

Later, when Eaton had the opportunity to describe this gentleman's uniform to some of the retired firefighters who had served in Fire Hall No. 1, those men confirmed that the description of the uniform sounded like the uniforms worn by firemen of the captain's day.

Both Wolfe and Eaton are serious people, with significant responsibilities for running this vast complex. Neither would impress as either prone to or capable of flights of fantasy, and it is apparent that their respective superiors have confidence in their abilities. In short, having spoken to several witnesses to this ghost, I must confess that I believe their descriptions of their experiences completely.

A BRAVE MAN DIES

On a Wednesday night in late February 1928, a fire broke out in "the trimming room" of McDorman Bridges Funeral Home on Dougherty Street. Capt. Peeler and his men of AFD Company No. 1 answered the call. In the smoke and confusion attendant to any emergency, Capt. Peeler walked into the open elevator doors on the ground floor of the funeral home and fell to the basement below. He may have been searching for survivors or answering a call for help which seemed to come from the other levels of the three-story building. We will never know why he took that fateful step, and one can only marvel at the heroism of a sixty-seven-year-old man still doing his duty in saving lives.

Capt. Peeler died of his injuries two days later. His funeral was held on Sunday at the First United Methodist Church, and fittingly, a fire truck from his company led the procession to his gravesite in Athens's Oconee Hills Cemetery. On February 26, the *Athens Banner Herald* memorialized him.

> Captain Peeler was with the Athens Fire Department
> for over a quarter of a century. He joined the volunteer
> department in 1881 and became a paid member in
> January of 1891. He was born in Clarke County,
> November 25, 1861. He was the oldest member of the
> Athens Fire Department at the time of his death, both
> from the standpoint of service and age.

Decades of change have transformed Athens's downtown area, and one doubts if Capt. Peeler would recognize the streets which he frequented in life. Buildings rise and fall with the passing years, and heating, water, and gas systems are now much safer and more reliable than in his day. Even the motor vehicles used to fight fires today would be almost unrecognizable to this local hero of yesteryear.

Still, the hardwood floors on the lower level of Fire Hall No. 1 are the same, and the basement storage area where the chief's fire wagon is sometimes stored during large events would seem familiar to a man of his time. The chief's wagon would represent a respite; a comforting sameness, a familiar thing.

With the bustle of modern Athens centered around this civic center and the many events there, it is comforting for us to know that a brave and dedicated man such as Capt. Peeler still keeps an eye on his beloved city. The whisper of his presence is still remembered and frequently felt in the fire hall where he dedicated his life to saving others.

A HAUNTED HANGAR

The evening light in the old hangar is dim, and the wind, whispering through the many cracks in the wall, sounds forlorn. The very openness of the lighted taxiways at the airport seem to betray a presence, and one can, all of a sudden, feel totally alone, even as the wind freshens. The hangar ghost is afoot. . . .

Ghosts, as everyone knows, should remain properly ensconced in grand houses with creaky hardwood floors, gloomy attics, and mysterious gables. Victorian buildings, with their rich, long histories, seem to be the proper settings for phantoms, which is why a modern, bustling airport strikes us as one of the least likely domiciles for any self-respecting spook. Still, the ghost of interest here has taken up residence in a hangar at the Athens-Ben Epps Airport, right alongside the most modern of twin-engine jets and single-engine planes.

This spooky resident has made himself known at the Athens airport in a cinder-block, round-top hangar built in 1942 or 1943. World War II was demanding large numbers of navy fliers, and during the war, flight instruction

The World War II "round-top"-style hangar is the oldest building at the Athens Ben Epps Airport. A ghostly spirit, perhaps that of a naval aviator trained here during the war, frequents the building late in the evening.

for thousands of young airmen took place at Georgia's first airport, which is located three miles east of Athens. Many fliers mastered their initial flying skills here, stayed briefly in Athens, and then were shipped out overseas.

The hangar is currently used for private flight training and maintenance. Sonny Smith, the proprietor of the flight school, is himself quite well known in Georgia aviation circles. It is frequently said that Smith has trained half the pilots in Athens, if not half the pilots in Georgia, and has forgotten more about aircraft than most pilots will ever know. Smith is well into his sixties is well known across the southeastern United States for his aviation exploits. He is as much myth as man to anyone who's been around airplanes in Georgia.

A PRANKSTER SPIRIT

In the late 1960s and early 1970s, Smith was flying businesspeople to various meetings around the southeast in his Piper Navaho, a medium-sized, cabin-class, twin-engine aircraft that seats two pilots and six passengers. Passengers and pilots alike board from a fuselage door behind the left wing. The aircraft cruises around two hundred to two hundred and twenty miles per hour, making it a popular and practical charter aircraft.

Smith had flown into the small Epps airfield three miles east of Athens around midnight one evening with a group of passengers from South Carolina and had another charter early the next morning. Chas Joyner, one of Smith's pilots, volunteered to clean up the aircraft so that Smith could go home and get some much-needed sleep. Joyner was alone in the unlighted end of the dark hangar and was using a flashlight to look over the Navaho. While cleaning the cockpit floor, Joyner clearly heard the door to Smith's private office open and then heard someone walk on the hangar's cement floor from the office to the open door of the aircraft behind the wing. Thinking it was Smith, he left the front of the aircraft and moved the four steps or so down the center isle to look out the door to find out what his boss wanted and perhaps to joke with Smith about missing his sleep. To his great surprise, there was nobody at the door.

Joyner thought that Smith was playing tricks on him in the darkened hangar, and he shouted something quite unprintable, as co-workers sometimes do. He returned to the cockpit to continue his cleaning. In a few minutes, he again heard steps on the concrete floor, so he moved back to the door, again expecting to see his boss. This time he took his flashlight and got to the aircraft door, he thought, just in time to shine the light directly into Smith's eyes. Imagine his surprise when, after hearing someone come in, no one was captured in the flashlight beam! Joyner got out of the aircraft and shone the light under the aircraft, expecting to see Smith's trademark cowboy boots. Again no one was in sight; no one was in the hangar at all!

Of course, airport hangars are large open areas, where multiple aircraft can be parked. Chas knew that if someone walked to the door of the plane on the concrete floor and then attempted to hide, he would still see their legs under the aircraft. In the open hangar, there would simply be no other place to hide. Also, Joyner heard no footsteps receding from the airplane when he went to the door to investigate.

At that point, Joyner was considerably nervous and decided to leave the hangar for the evening. He did manage to lock the hangar on his way out, with the aircraft only partially clean. To this day, Chas Joyner will not go in Smith's hangar alone at night. While Joyner is not prone to fears—and everyone agrees that his flying nerve is unsurpassed—he simply prefers to do his late-night maintenance without any ghosts about.

OTHER MYSTERIES

Of course, were that the only occurrence, this ghost would be one of many apparitions who apparently materialize only once. However, various other airport employees reported sightings of a young man sitting in the hangar late at night or the sound of doors slamming mysteriously.

John Brewer, an accomplished pilot well known for his flight instruction, flying skills, and good judgment, worked as an instructor for Smith for a number of years in the 1990s. He was alone in an inner office of the hangar one day when he heard the door to the outer office slam in an unusually loud fashion. Given the pranksters that frequent any general aviation airport, Brewer assumed that someone had entered prepared to joke with whoever happened to be around, so Brewer shouted, "I'm in here." When no one entered the inner office, Brewer walked to the outer office to see if, perhaps, a new student pilot or a customer was visiting. To his shock, he found that that the door he had heard slam was wide open! The chills in his spine came then, and he recalled the stories about the hangar ghost from other pilots. He shut the door and went about his business.

This airport ghost is interesting for a number of reasons. Not only does he appear in a setting that most would not associate with ghosts, but his antics have been experienced by a group of highly practical people. Fliers are trained to be reasonable, to make judgments based on data, to depend on technology in adverse conditions, and to manage stressful situations without panic. They tend to be highly practical, somewhat mechanically minded persons. Sonny Smith, as one example, is well regarded not only as a pilot but as a highly skilled aircraft mechanic. Certainly the several aviators mentioned in this brief synopsis are all highly skilled aviators and well regarded by their peers. Each of these gentlemen has flown professionally, logging literally thousands of hours in all types of aircraft, from the smallest trainers to charter jets. Each is known as a competent decision-maker, not prone to hasty judgments, personal fears, or phobias. Each has managed aircraft in tough weather and adverse flying circumstances in which numerous lives depended on their skills and good judgment. These are not highly impressionable folks, and wouldn't generally be expected to either tell stories of the supernatural or to believe such stories. In spite of the practical-mindedness, I've heard Smith tell his ghostly experience to groups of pilots and passengers sitting around his hangar lounge, and this story, in such an unlikely location, is what makes this spook so intriguing.

RESEARCHING THE SPIRIT

I questioned a number of people who work at Athens-Ben Epps. Some had not heard of a ghost at the airport, while some had but were reluctant to talk about it. Some say the ghost appears in a uniform of some sort, and this would suggest that this ghost is one of the thousands of navy airmen who trained here in WW II. Those flyers served all over the world and many, no doubt, lost their lives in foreign skies in service to their country. The history behind this hypothesis would seem to be right, in that the hangar was built early in the war, and much of the training for these flyers would have taken place in the same cinderblock building Smith is still using.

However, Smith himself has another theory as to the ghost's identify.

BEN EPPS: A MAN OF HISTORY

Within four years of the Wright brother's historic first flight of a heavier-than-air, machine-powered aircraft at Kitty Hawk, North Carolina, in the winter of 1903, Ben Epps had built and flown his own "flying machine" in

Aviation pioneer Ben Epps in his Athens shop.

Athens at the future site of Georgia's first airport, which today bears his name. He constructed his 1907 Monoplane at his workshop on Washington Street. (Some point after World War II, a second, smaller airport was located in Athens, with the main runway running down what is now Baxter Street, just east of the intersection with Alps Road. However, that airport closed within ten years, with the expansion of the city of Athens.)

Beginning in 1917, Epps made a career of charter services and aviation instruction until he crashed in Athens in 1937. Epps and a student pilot died of injuries sustained when the engine of their light biplane failed and the plane crashed on take-off. Ironically and tragically, the first fatality at the airport was the man who both had founded Georgia's first airport and brought aviation to the state.

It is interesting to note that the hangar was not built when Epps died in 1937, but only later during WW II, sometime in 1942 or 1943. Would this suggest that the resident ghost may be the spirit of someone besides Epps?

WHO IS THIS SPIRIT?

In short, there have been enough experiences from employees and visitors to the airport to document this haunting, for those will to suspend their disbelief in apparitions. Still, we don't know much about this ghost, and much of the information above involves supposition. By all accounts, this is a relatively benign specter who doesn't intentionally scare people and only makes his presence known occasionally. In contrast, there is also no evidence of this ghost helping folks, as is sometimes the case in various hauntings. This ghost merely goes about his business of visiting the hangar late at night—slamming doors or loudly striding across the floor as he goes about his ghostly rounds—and materializing in shadowy form only occasionally.

Still, when I think of the specter at the hangar, I like to picture a substantive man of history—a leader, an innovator, and a doer. Epps was center stage in early aviation, and in the nebulous twilight after his unexpected death, he may have chosen to linger here a while. Given Epps dedication to and love for aviation, he may occasionally show up at his beloved eponymous airport. This apparition may visit the site of his contributions to early aviation, flying career, personal glory, and ultimately, his premature demise. He may well prefer to spend leisurely time here on dark evenings, when the Athens moon hangs low over the runways he used so frequently in life. He would ignore the newer jets as uninteresting, but he may well linger in some hidden corner of the oldest hangar on the field, experiencing again the smell of gasoline in the tip tanks, feeling the prop-wash, or checking engine oil in some Cessna trainer—perhaps even supervise Smith in changing a spark plug or two.

Buried in a double-plot with his wife, their shared tombstone proclaims that "he inspired generations to fly and together they taught their children to soar." So who could blame Epps if he chose to stay close to his airport and the things he had loved in life?

GHOSTS AT AN AIRPORT?

The ghost at the Athens-Ben Epps Airport is apparently not the only aviation facility in Georgia which experiences hauntings. The small town of Douglas shares a history similar to that of Athens in that World War II airmen were trained at that city's airport also. Today an examiner for the Federal Aviation Authority does pilot-check flights from the field in Douglas, and many new student pilots, as well as veteran pilots from nearby Athens, complete their check flights and competency flights there.

On that field in Douglas, pilots tell of a ghostly guest named McGee. Apparently, McGee survived World War II and tried to build a career in aviation in the late 1940s around this small town in Coffee County. However, like many veterans who had seen too much horror in the war, he never seemed to get his life moving forward after returning home. He eventually hanged himself in an aircraft shed at the Douglas Municipal Airport, and he is now frequently heard slamming doors or rocking in one of the rocking chairs on the porch. Even sunny days when no wind is blowing, the corner rocker can be seen to rock for no apparent reason.

My wife, nervous before her own FAA-required competency check flight in the fall of 2001, was completing her pre-flight planning when a door in the hangar slammed loudly. The gentleman working with her calmly stated, "You just met McGee." Then he told her the story of McGee's suicide in the hangar. Needless to say, from my wife's perspective, this story was not the most relaxing thing to hear immediately prior to her flight. This story from southeast Georgia is presented to show that ghosts do sometimes hang out at airports. (In spite of this mini-trauma, my wife scored just fine on her flight.)

THE WEDDING CAKE HOUSE

A HAUNTED SORORITY

Co-written with S. DeLeigh Pearce

Apparitions often come from tragedy, and one of the best known in Athens apparently resulted from a tragic suicide just before the dawning of the twentieth century. A large, older home, now used as the home for the Alpha Gamma Delta sorority on Milledge Avenue, has become noted as the home of the spirit of Susie Carithers who hanged herself there, in the attic, on her wedding day. Built in 1896 by civil engineer, architect, and businessman William Winstead Thomas, the house was acquired by James Yancey Carithers in 1913 as a wedding present for his daughter Susie. In fact, the two-story frame house looks very much like a layered wedding cake, standing on the corner of Milledge Avenue and Baxter Street.

DeLeigh Pearce, one of the officers of Alpha Gamma, had a recent experience with this apparition and tells the following story. In 2001, she had lived in the house only two weeks and was in the television room (one of the first floor rooms of the sorority house) with her roommate studying, when she first heard

The delicate Beaux Arts detailing of the circa 1896-Thomas-Carithers House has earned it the local nickname of the "Wedding Cake House." *LOCs*

a "scraping noise" from upstairs, in the attic.

"As the noise began, I looked up at my roommate, Lauren, studying on the couch across from me. We were the only two Alpha Gamma sisters in our house that Thursday night since there was a party at a fraternity house down the street," Pearce explained. "All was eerily quiet except for this scraping, sliding sound, and Lauren frowned as she looked back at me. She smiled a tiny, tight-lipped smile as if to say, 'No way.' And then came the footsteps, soft and light, cutting through the silence of the house—footsteps overhead, pushing a chair.

"By this time I had forgotten all about my studying, and was staring at Lauren with wide eyes, goose-flesh rising on the back of my arms.

"'I don't believe this,' I whispered to her. The words had no sooner left my mouth than we heard the final loud crash, as the chair toppled over upstairs. Lauren jumped up instantly, as all of the lights in the downstairs part of the house suddenly cut off, leaving us alone in the dark house. Then there was only the sound of our footsteps, mine and Lauren's, as we ran out of our house screaming."

The Wedding Cake House has been the residence of the women of Alpha Gamma Delta sorority since 1939. Fashioned in the style of a two-tiered wedding cake, the house is quite beautiful, featuring delicate floral-patterned friezes and Ionic columns in each room that give the home a feminine feel. But perhaps the crowning glory of the house are the leaded glass windows designed by Tiffany Studios which flank the recessed front door and which are currently insured by Lloyd's of London for one million dollars each. The sorority sisters have numerous black-and-white photos of Susie Carithers playing a piano that her father had designed to accommodate her love of song. Still, many feel that the true uniqueness of this home is the spirit within.

GHOSTLY MANIFESTATIONS EVERY YEAR

Stories from no less than six AΓΔ sisters who were living in the house during the 2001–2002 academic year reflect the continued presence of Susie. Lauren Grillo not only shared the experience described above, but also had an unusual experience of her own in the upstairs bathroom in December 2001. When she went to wash her face, she noticed through an opaque shower door a figure dressed in white standing in the shower. Lauren said hello and began to wash her face. Realizing in a moment that she had received no response, she then decided to ignore the person in the shower and left the bathroom.

However, becoming more curious a moment later, she returned and the figure was gone. Of course, no one had entered or left the bathroom; Grillo had not gotten that far before turning back, and was never out of sight of the bathroom door. She thinks now that this was another visit from Susie.

Two women, Shay Virture and Lauren Sessons, live in the Hideaway, an upstairs room on the north side of the older section of the house which was originally used as the butler's room. The room has service call buttons located in it, which connected the room to all the other rooms in the house. Both Virture and Sessons heard the "scratching" sounds such as those described by Pearce above, as well as gentle moaning sounds that seemed to come from the attic directly upstairs which sounded like a young girl crying.

Virture is a night owl and is frequently up until 4:00 A. M., often the last person awake in the house. On one occasion in January 2002, she went in to the bathroom adjacent to her bedroom very late one evening to brush her teeth and clean her face before retiring. She was washing her face with a warm-water washcloth, and when she looked up she saw in the mirror above the sink, the figure of a young woman standing immediately behind her. When she turned, the figure was gone, and in fairly short order so was Virture. She ran into her bedroom, very upset, and locked the door; she slept with the lights on that evening.

On another occasion, Virture saw a shadowy figure walk past the door to the Hideaway, and also felt a chill as the apparition passed. Because of these and other experiences, Virture is "deathly afraid" of this bathroom. So much so that when brushing her teeth, she wets her toothbrush under the bathroom faucet, applies toothpaste to the brush, and leaves the bathroom entirely, returning to her own bedroom across the hall to actually brush.

Loren Sessons states that the door to their room, the Hideaway, is very difficult to get shut entirely, and requires some effort to do so. However, when no one is around, the door will frequently pop open by itself.

SUSIE'S DEATH

The stories of Susie Carither's unhappy wedding day are handed down from generation to generation of AΓΔ sisters. According to the legends, Susie's wedding was to be held in this house, and all the elite of Athens' society were in attendance. However, on the day that had been anticipated for so long, a huge storm engulfed most of Clarke County and North Georgia. Despite the storm, they made it to the new house on Milledge Avenue, determined not to miss the huge social event. The wedding was scheduled for four o'clock in the afternoon, but Susie was ready long before that, a vision of loveliness in her long satin gown.

Susie's groom was traveling from farther away than most of her guests, having been out of town on the night before the wedding, and the bridge he needed to take to get into Athens was down because of the incredible storm. Susie grew more and more anxious with the passing time. By five o'clock, over an hour after the wedding ceremony was to have begun, the guests began to say their quiet good-byes.

While her parents stood in the lavishly decorated foyer trying to conceal their humiliation, no one noticed as Susie slipped up the grand staircase. Moments later the guests heard the sound of a chair scraping overhead—the same sound the girls of the sorority still hear years later. They then heard the chair topple to the floor and everyone in the room below instinctively knew what Susie had done. The suicide by hanging took place in the attic, directly above the room which would have been Susie's bedroom after her wedding (later known as the Engagement Room). Ironically, Susie's groom made it to the wedding just as her body was being taken from the attic.

RECENT HAUNTINGS

The sightings and experiences of this particular ghost seem limited to several of the original rooms on the north side of the house, including the television room and the piano room on the first floor. Weird things have been seen also in several bedrooms, a hallway, and a bathroom, which are directly upstairs from these two downstairs rooms. Several sorority sisters have commented on the fact that no apparitions have been experienced in any of the southern rooms, even though those rooms, like the rooms to the north, are original to the house and date from the original construction of 1896. Apparently, Susie prefers familiar terrain.

Year after year, Alpha Gamma sisters have noticed a trend among women who have lived in the Engagement Room. It seems that nearly every year at least one girl who lives in this room is lavaliered (given a necklace with a fraternity boy's Greek letters to symbolize that the couple is "going steady") by her sweetheart. The process is a celebration but it is very serious and it doesn't happen

This is the attic in which, legend holds, bride-to-be Susie Carithers hanged herself in the 1910s. This attic is directly over the northeast corner of the house where most of the hauntings now occur.

often. The tradition of the Engagement Room has been passed down from 1939 until now, with sorority sisters in that room making these important commitments each year. The women who live in this house believe that the power of the Engagement Room is quite strong because of the spirit of Susie Carithers. Perhaps Susie is trying to play cupid in the lives of others, as a response to her lost love and tragic end.

Sisters throughout the house tell of flickering lights or of hearing piano music drifting out of the piano room late at night. The girls often tell their stories with a smile, some believing in Susie more than others. However, almost everyone has encountered something in this house that wasn't "quite right," whether they saw a glimpse of a pale face in the attic window, or heard the all too common sound of a chair scraping overhead.

Holly McCorale was in the house alone around midnight one weekend evening in 2001, and was preparing for bed in the middle front bedroom on the second floor. She began to hear a whimper, then a definite moaning which she described as a gentle and quietly persuasive crying, but she could not pinpoint the source. The noise got louder and became recognizable as a female crying. As McCorale reported, "Not hysterical crying, just an incredibly sad crying." She explored the hallway and other rooms next to hers, but could not fine the source of the sound. She returned to her room and began to read a bit, but the moaning returned, getting louder and louder. She then locked the door, and when a roommate telephoned a bit later, McCorale invited her to come home—quickly!

She was, by this time, much too excited to sleep and began to read again. A bit later she felt a presence beside her in the room. "To me, it was like somebody was sitting next to me in that room. It was an eerie feeling," she said.

McCorale had never believed in the sightings of Susie before, thinking that these legends of Susie were part of the kind of folklore common to any sorority. Still, after this experience, McCorale reports that she is definitely now a believer in ghosts. As she herself explained, "You couldn't *pay* me to spend the night in that attic!"

In response to these minor manifestations—the moaning, the scraping of a chair across the floor, the popping-open of doors, the flickering lights, and such—many sorority sisters will say rather loudly, "Susie, please stop!" At that, the unwanted manifestations usually come to an end. However, not all of the manifestations are this benign.

TWO WOMEN SEE SUSIE'S SPIRIT

Perhaps the most terrifying recent apparition was witnessed by ΑΓΔ sister and house resident Ashley Holt. Holt getting ready to go out for the evening in September 2001. Her roommate Ann came into their shared bedroom quite excited, yelling, "Ashley, come down here! You have to see this!" Ann dragged Ashley down the stairs that wrap around the west end of the foyer in the original home, with three separate sections of stairs from the second floor to the first floor.

Ashley got to the middle section of the stairs and heard the piano playing. Looking through the door into the television room and the adjacent door to the piano room, Holt and her roommate both saw the apparition of a young woman playing the piano. Holt described the woman as dressed in white with lace around her wrists and arms, as well as a veil over her face. Holt stated that, "It was the scariest thing. I started screaming."

The entire sorority heard Holt scream as she and her roommate ran sobbing back upstairs, and both wanted to leave the house as quickly as possible. Of course, that brought the entire house to inquire; the women told their sisters that they had seen Susie. However, when the two returned downstairs only moments later with their housemates, the room was quiet and the piano was deserted. Holt reported that she had never had any similar experiences in her life, but that she now believes in ghosts.

Neither Holt or her roommate slept at the sorority house that night, and the

As the ill-fated Susie Carithers did generations before her, an Alpha Gamma Delta sister enjoys playing the piano in the music room of the Wedding Cake House.

sisters left behind were all skittish of this apparition and the frequently flickering shadows on the walls.

A painting of the Wedding Cake House hangs in the foyer of the house itself. The painting was given to Alpha Gamma Delta in 1996, on the one-hundredth anniversary of the construction of the house. Members of Alpha Kappa Psi fraternity, located directly across Milledge Avenue from AΓΔ, found the painting in the attic of their own house.

Their legends suggest that the painting was done years ago by a young autistic boy who spent his days in the attic. His only view of the outside world was that of the Wedding Cake House, and so he painted it as he saw it from his attic window. It is a fairly large painting, and definitely shows a downward view of the Wedding Cake House.

On the night that the painting was given to the sorority, Athens was once again engulfed in a great storm. The next morning, the sorority sisters noticed that a single droplet of water had fallen on the painting, leaving a slight drip mark on the canvas from the top of the attic where Susie hanged herself, through the Engagement Room, and down to the painted grass below. The sisters of Alpha Gamma Delta then checked the ceiling above for leaks, and found none. Today the pale streak can still be found on the painting, left some say, by the tears of Susie on the one-hundredth anniversary of the house where she meet her end.

Across town, in the Oconee Hills Cemetery, near the top of the hill in the older section of this hallowed ground, one can find numerous graves of various Carithers, but records reveal no Susie, Susan, or Thomas Carithers interred there. The records for Oconee Hills were destroyed by fire and were then re-created by cataloging the names and death dates from headstones; this left many graves unrecorded, and throughout the older part of the cemetery, one can find numerous grave-length depressions with no marker at all.

How does one interpret the lack of a marker? As the record keeper indicated, "That doesn't mean she isn't here." Also a check of cemetery records of six Clarke County-area counties showed no Susie or Susan Carithers living in the appropriate timeframe. Still, tragic suicides were not subjects to be discussed in polite company in the early days of the last century, and one may easily imagine that the grave of a suicide may have been left unmarked intentionally.

Susie's final resting place remains a mystery.

Today, the young women of the AΓΔ house still enjoy the stately rooms, the wide staircase, and the luxury of living in a late-nineteenth-century mansion. Some have their reservations concerning Susie, but many who had previously never experienced anything of a haunted nature are now confirmed believers in this apparition. It is difficult to tell where legend ends and actual manifestation experiences begin in this particular story. Still, the fear expressed by many young women is obvious, and through their interviews, it became apparent that this is a real—that is to say—a very serious fear for some of these women.

Whether it's a flash of white behind them as they check their reflection in an antique mirror, the flickering of lights, the sonorous sounds of piano music, the unexpected opening of doors, or the barely audible moaning of a young woman, Susie's existence in this house is, for many of the sisters, as real as their own. These women believe that the spirit of Susie Carithers still resides in the Wedding Cake House. At the very least, the sisters of Alpha Gamma Delta live with an interesting set of tales and the incredible, palpable sadness of a young girl from nearly a hundred years ago, crying out—as if reaching for a love she herself was denied—touches their hearts today.

SPIRITS OF THE BARROW-TATE HOUSE

While enjoying an evening in one of the most historic houses in Athens, one can almost hear the hoofbeats of horses unseen, the creaking of carriage wheels that are there no more. One can almost sense the helpful spirit of York as he reassures the old woman, the woman who was once the young mistress of the house. York is quiet now, if present at all, and the old house is well situated for yet another generation of the family. For six generations, there has been no mortgage on this house, and it has been in the hands of the same family—how often is that true for any house in America? But the house is also in the hands of one of the more famous ghosts in Athens.

The spirit is that of a man named York, who served as a yard man for William Tate and his wife Susan Barrow Tate at this most famous of Athens houses. York lovingly tended the wisteria, azaleas, and camellias for decades in the early years of the twentieth century; the gardens were exquisite then by all accounts and many meetings of University of Georgia officials were held there. After his death, Susan Tate was known to experience York's presence, often while sitting on the back porch of the house. The lot is quite extensive, though somewhat overgrown at present; it needs again York's loving hand.

THIS HISTORIC HOUSE

The Barrow-Tate House has been described as one of the most architecturally significant houses in Athens, as well as one the most haunted. Still, aside from spirits, the house has a rich history. The house was built in 1878 by Pope Barrow and served as a family homeplace for many years. For many years in the mid-1900s, every University of Georgia student was aware of the fact that UGA Dean of Men William Tate lived there with his wife, Susan. Many of Georgia's older living alumni well remember the caring influence of Dean Tate and more recent alumni enjoy the student center which bears his name.

Born on September 21, 1903 in north Georgia, Tate attended the university in the 1920s. For over five decades, his concern for both town and gown was felt, as he served as an instructor, assistant dean, dean of men, and university and community philanthropist. Dean Tate served the University through seven presidential administrations.

According to Susan Tate, two different ghosts live in the family's rambling old house at 436 Dearing Street. Ms. Tate reported many unexplained experiences in the house, which were recorded by Nancy Roberts in her book *Georgia Ghosts*. Until she took up residence in a nursing home in the mid-1990s, Ms. Tate had spent her entire life in the house, recalling many sounds which were unexplained, sounds such as the rattle of wheels on boards, or horse hooves in the nearby street

This historic house, once a showplace, has been in the same family for six generations, and at least two spirits have been noted here over the years.

at night when no horses or carriages were present.

Ms. Tate also reported that she was once visited by a deceased African-American gentleman yardman named York, who had worked as a yardman for the family for many years. As Ms Tate struggled with a difficult personal decision, the specter appeared to her with a message of peace and assurance.

"As children, we would walk along with York and ask him questions while he worked. He was always patient with us," Ms. Tate recalled.

"York had been dead for many years, yet there he stood, holding his hat in his hands while he looked over at me," she continued. "He said quite clearly in the kind way he always spoke, 'It's going to be alright, little missy.' Then he disappeared."

Ms. Tate also reported a sighting of an apparition she believes is her father by a university student. Running into Ms. Tate one day, the student inquired about the older man with a beard she often saw sitting on the front porch of the Tate house. Ms. Tate replied that no older, bearded men lived with the family, but she believes that the spirit of her father—dead for many years—was present in the old house.

AN EVENING WITH A SOUTHERN GENTLEMAN

I rode over to this house one rainy evening, little suspecting that I would be greeted by a family member. To my surprise, Jonathan Tate opened the door to me, and before I could explain my presence, he graciously invited us in. Jonathan is Dean Tate's son, and the great-grandson of David Barrow (UGA Class of 1874), who later served as chancellor of the university.

Over the next several hours, I spent one of the most interesting and pleasant evenings of my life with him, enjoying the presence of a true Southern gentleman. Not only was Jonathan's accent distinctly pleasing, his culture and refined sensibilities were evident early in the conversation.

Within an hour—and after a few fine beers—Jonathan looked at me directly and said, "So what did you come for?" Of course I mentioned that I had an interest in ghosts, and so Jonathan shared with me several of the stories of the hauntings in the old house.

Because Jonathan has had no experiences recently, we cannot be certain that the spirit of York is still present in the house. Perhaps York has found his peace and left the land he so lovingly tended for so long.

THE GREAT ORATOR OF DEMOSTHENIAN HALL

Demosthenian Hall is the fourth oldest building on the campus of the University of Georgia, and simply looks spooky. Constructed in 1824, the building has a rich history, so one would almost expect it to hold various ghostly manifestations and, according to numerous reports, spirits do indeed reside here. Nestled as it is within the great oaks and sprawling lawns in the oldest section of campus, stepping into the hall can give one the

The Toombs Oak and the University of Georgia Chapel, circa 1900. *University of Georgia Libraries*

Demosthenian Hall faces the north campus quadrangle of the University of Georgia. *LOC*

sensation of walking back in time. Replete with large rooms and high ceilings, the formal, Federal-style building has a dis-tinctively eerie feel even when well fully lit. Many members of the Demosthenian Literary Society head-quartered there have felt a presence—perhaps a spirit—there.

In the early 1800s, a University of Georgia education was all-consuming, with long days spent in classes and evenings in discussion in this early univer-sity building. The Demosthenian Literary Society was organized in 1803, only

Robert Toombs at age seventy-five.

three years after classes began at the Uni-versity of Georgia (then called Franklin College), placing its roots deep within the history of the university. Named in honor of the ancient Greek orator, statesmen, and champion of democracy Demos-thenes, the group focuses on public speaking and debate. This revered meeting house has served as think tank, study society, and social center for students at the University of Georgia from that early period until today. It has witnessed the transitions in collegiate study for over 180 years, ranging from candlelit discus-sion of ancient philosophy to latte-powered blogging on the internet.

The ghost associated with Demosthenian Hall is, by all accounts, the ghost of U.S. Senator and Confederate Secretary of State Robert Augustus Toombs (1810–1885) Ghostly manifestations of Toombs abound in the ancient hall. Members of the DLS report hearing footsteps pacing in the upper chamber, some have felt a "presence" on dark evenings, and still others have even seen a gray apparition on the ancient stairway. These manifestations are quite common for ghosts who may be tied to several specific places.

Robert Toombs was, in life, quite an interesting and complicated character. One can find in this man a scholar, a drunkard, a politician, a statesman, a general, a devoted husband, an affluent attorney, and a doting father; surely an unusual list of conflicting personality traits. Reared in Wilkes County, Georgia, only forty miles east of Athens, Robert Toombs came within a hair's breath of election as the first (and only) president of the Confederate States of America. He did serve the Confederate States of America as its secretary of state and sub-

A corner of the Assembly Room of Demosthenian Hall. *LOC*

sequently as a general in the Confederate army. Many years prior to that he had been a student at the university from 1824 to 1828.

During his studies in Athens, Toombs flagrantly violated one university policy after another. In an age when proper behavior and exquisite manners were the tradition of all gentlemen who attended the university, young Robert was always in trouble for drinking excessively or for the shameful use of tobacco. It has been documented that he spend some time in the Eagle Tavern in lower Clarke County—a den of whisky and sin, according to many of the professors at UGA in the 1800s.

Toombs constantly found himself in opposition to his professors, in an age in which students were not generally encouraged to think for themselves. Consequently, only a few months prior to his anticipated graduation, he was expelled from the university. He may well have been the first student so disciplined. As UGA historian Nash Boney described it, Toombs went three years "breaking every rule in the book and then arguing eloquently for one more chance, but finally he departed, claiming that he resigned a split second before President Waddel could expel him.

Toombs was notably upset when he was expelled and made immediate plans to get even with the university. On what would have been his graduation day in 1828, Toombs waited until the commencement services were in progress in the Chapel which sits beside Demosthenian Hall. Assured of his notable oratory skills, Toombs stood under a large oak tree, between the Chapel and Demosthenian Hall and began to deliver a grand oration as the commencement ceremony continued in the adjacent building. Tradition holds that Toombs was so eloquent and charismatic that the entire Chapel emptied.

At some later point, the oak tree beside Demosthenian Hall under which he spoke was named the Toombs Oak in his honor. While the tree is long gone, a historic marker presently marks that hallowed spot beside the DLS headquarters.

As it turns out, his university days were not the only time Toombs was noted for his oratory skills or his vocal opposition to ideas with which he disagreed. Even though expelled from the University of Georgia, he continued his studies elsewhere and then lead a long and distinguished career in state and national politics, serving in the Georgia legislature and then the U.S. House of Representatives and U.S. Senate.

When Abraham Lincoln was elected president of the United States in 1860, Robert Toombs became a vocal supporter of the secession of the South. He was so passionate in his oratory that he was named to serve as secretary of state in the only presidential administration of the Confederate States of America, under President Jefferson Davis, a post which lasted only five months. He subsequently joined the CSA army as a brigadier general and lead an important defense of one section of the Confederate line in a critical battle at Antietam Creek. Here also, he became a vocal opponent of the leadership, and subsequently, left that position after a brief time.

Toombs, according to Boney, "spent most of the rest of the war holed up in Georgia, denouncing the Davis administration in Richmond and inadvertently damaging the Confederate war effort." After the war, Toombs fled to Havana and London to avoid arrest and returned to Georgia to become one of the state's most thoroughly unreconstructed rebels. Strangely, even though his expulsion could not have been a pleasant memory for Toombs, he always remained loyal to the University of Georgia, and even served quite proudly on the University Board of Trustees from 1859 until his death in 1885.

The manifestations of the spirit which now haunts Demosthenian Hall began on the day of Toombs' death. Tradition holds that on the day Toombs died, a powerful lightning bolt struck the Toombs Oak, which grew adjacent to Demosthenian Hall. After the tree died, the remaining members of the Demosthenian Literary Society cut the stump down and placed it inside the hall as a reminder of this fiery orator. Members use this stump as a pedestal when they seek office in the society. Perhaps Robert Toombs is attracted to the mighty oak which honored him in life for over fifty years.

With this colorful character as the ghost-in-residence, current members of the DLS may well feel a bit apprehensive when studying alone in the hall at night. DLS member Carl Pyrdum reported, "I have felt when I was studying really late, this sense of someone telling me to 'get out' and I've left, but I've heard other members say when they've gotten that feeling, they've told Bob, 'No!' and the feeling went away." In spite of the discomfort sometimes caused by this spirit, most members of the society, when they experience an uneasy feeling late at night or hear creaky floorboards in the upper chamber with no one else around, simply take this now-famous spirit as a source of inspiration

Toombs spent his later years in his home in Washington, Georgia, and died in1885. The room in which Toombs died has been refurbished and decorated with period furniture, much of which belonged to Toombs himself. Standing by the bed in which Toombs passed away over one hundred and fifteen years ago, walking in his garden, and reviewing the historic relics from this man's life, one can only marvel at the inconsistencies in his character. Perhaps individuals with obvious and numerous inconsistencies tend to manifest themselves as apparitions—perhaps to finish some unfinished business not dealt with in life.

Toombs was buried in a quiet family plot in the Rest Haven Cemetery in Washington, Georgia, but his spirit seems to prefer the comfort and familiarity of his beloved Demosthenian Hall, near the remains of the Toombs Oak and the site of his great oration.

DO SPIRITS TRAVEL?:
THE GHOST OF ROBERT TOOMBS

In addition to the stately assembly hall of University of Georgia's Demosthenian Literary Society, Robert Toombs apparently also manifests himself occasionally in his ancestral home in Washington, Georgia.

When refurbishing the Toombs House in Washington, Georgia, several workmen reported a strange tapping in an upstairs rooms. One man decided to investigate the noise and because the once-grand house had deteriorated to the point where small animals were frequent visitors, he half expected to find a squirrel or some other animal in residence. When the workman went upstairs, he realized the noise came from the northeast corner bedroom, the room in which Toombs died in 1885. However, the worker could find no animal or any other logical explanation. An eerie feeling came over the workman, who subsequently refused to work alone upstairs. Within a two weeks, this workman had chosen other employment and refused to work in the Toombs House at all.

This ghostly manifestation in the Toombs House raises an interesting point: Robert Toombs may exemplify a spirit that travels, or at least manifests itself in two different locations which were important in life. While many ghosts seem attracted to one location or object, there are examples of ghosts who appear in various places, and the Toombs apparition seems to fit that category.

The rambling old Toombs house is redolent of the years between 1867 and 1885 when Toombs was in residence there. Relegated to unimportant obscurity by his refusal to take an oath of loyalty to the United States, as former Confederate soldiers were required to, Toombs lived in the house, practiced law, and generally served as a model local citizen. He outlived his wife of fifty years by approximately seven years and, to his death, was an "unreconstructed rebel." He died a lonely old man, ignored and irrelevant, and is buried in Washington, Georgia.

It is interesting to reflect on this crusty old man, this man of contradictions. One cold day in Washington, Georgia, I stood by his grave and said a prayer for this restless spirit; that brought a sense of closure to this story for me. Still, I think I would like to share a brandy and an evening's conversation with him. It might not be totally pleasant, but great ideas were often debated at his table, and in many ways some of the history of the Old South as determined there.

"Unreconstructed Rebel" Robert Toombs was born in, died in, and continues to haunt his namesake house in Washington, Georgia, as he does his beloved Demosthenian Hall at the University of Georgia. Spirits apparently can travel to various locations they loved in life. *1892*

Even in his declining years, he never wished to be "reconstructed" and his spirit seems to roam in several beloved spots, bespeaking a rugged energy and rage at the outcome of history. When I contemplate this spirit, I sense a longing, a restlessness, and I pray that this great orator, this leader, and this highly unusual character may eventually find peace for himself.

THE GHOST TAVERN

Walking into the dimly lit cellar of the Eagle Tavern in Watkinsville, Georgia, one moves from bright sunshine into a dank world of malodorous decay, ancient spirits, ghostly apparitions, and perhaps even a portal to the supernatural. There is only a mud-and-rock floor and foundation walls of ancient brick—no clutter and virtually nothing in storage in this six-foot-high space. The joists for the first floor have been insulated over the preceding fifty years, but the dank smell of the wet dirt floor leaves a musty odor and an uneasy feeling. . . .

Four or five paces from the door, there is a quite different, more unsettling odor; the stench of decay; the odor of death. The smell is very specifically localized; only noticeable in that particular spot. Only a few feet further into the cellar, and the odor is gone; a few paces more and again the smell of death returns. It is chilling to know one has smelled a ghost. Indeed, with a fetid ghost in the basement, a Confederate soldier downstairs, and a trio of spirits upstairs, the Eagle Tavern may well be the most haunted building in north Georgia.

This rough-cut lumber structure, dating from 1789, is a prime location for ghosts, and the oldest building in the Athens area doesn't disappoint. In the 1780s and 1790s, Watkinsville, then called Big Springs, was the county seat of Clarke County (Oconee County was created from lower Clarke after the Civil War). The historic building served as a frontier fort from 1789 until around 1800, when the building was remodeled as a roadhouse and tavern. Still, the ghosts are the important thing. . . .

Anita Rekli, director of tourism for Oconee County, whose office is in the Eagle Tavern, has an interest in spirits. Indeed, she hosted the first Oconee County Ghost Tour in the fall of 2001. Rekli noted many unusual happenings in the building when she worked in the tavern late at night, including hearing old chains moving by themselves and various unexplained noises. During her first year as tourism director, many self-proclaimed psychics visited the tavern and each one has told her that ghosts were plentiful in this old building.

"It is said there are three ghosts upstairs and then one ghost in the parlor," Rikli reports. "A lady told me that there's also a ghost in the basement, so there may be five, but I'm told of four here inside the lodge. There's a ghost of an elderly lady upstairs. There's one of a man and then a child, but they're not

The Eagle Tavern may be home to at least six ghosts. One employee will not work in the tavern alone at night. *LOC*

related—I've had actually three different people tell me that, who didn't know each other. They just walked in and the first thing they said when they came in the door was, 'You have ghosts in the tavern.' We have a ghost in the parlor [the southernmost downstairs room] who stands in front of the fireplace."

Rekli continued her oration concerning the numerous people who have told her of their ghostly experiences in the Eagle Tavern, and it was apparent that merely sorting out all of these restless spirits would be a considerable problem. Clearly, this ancient building has many stories to tell.

Another employee of the Eagle Tavern, who I'll call Janie, is very nervous about the female spirit who haunts the upstairs rooms of the inn. In particular, this spirit is most noticeable between the upstairs rooms, as well as on the stairs. Janie reports that "I don't go upstairs when I'm here by myself. Basically the upstairs doorway freaks me out, and I won't walk downstairs with my back towards the upstairs. I walk down sideways. It just makes me feel better to have something behind my back."

Janie noted that she was something of a psychic herself and then described the gender of the spirit in the upstairs doorway. "Whatever is in the doorway, I feel like it's feminine," she says. "I kind of got the feeling that there is a man here too."

After noting that she is a practicing Christian, Janie continues, "I mostly think that there is a reason why they are here, and there's a reason why either God put them here or why Satan's put them here. Some are here for good and some are here for evil, and I don't really know if there's something there—if it's my imagination or not—but it doesn't give me a good feeling. I've got no problem walking into this [downstairs]. It's the upstairs doorway; the rooms don't bother me."

THE OLD TAVERN

Although the building had many functions throughout its long life—tavern, seventeen-bed hotel, stagecoach stop, general store, storage house, and museum—the structure began life in 1789 as a fortification, referred to at that time as Fort Edwards. It was built to protect the local white population from the Oconee tribe of the Creek nation and included rifle slits instead of windows, as well as a defensible water source in the basement. This well, now filled in, still figures prominently in stories of the supernatural at the Eagle Tavern.

Once the perceived Creek threat was gone, the building was transformed into a roadhouse. Sitting immediately across the street from the Big Springs courthouse and serving as the main hotel for Clarke County, the Eagle Tavern in 1801 was a prime meeting place for local politicians, judges riding their circuit, and other community leaders. Many notables stayed in this tavern, including the poet Sidney Lanier and Confederate General Robert Toombs. When five early political leaders came from the Georgia capital of Louisville to Big Springs on horseback in June 1801, to scout a location for the recently funded university—later known as the "Ride of the Senatus Academicus (Academic Decree)" or the "Ride of Five"—tradition holds that the group stopped briefly at the Eagle Tavern.

Until well into the 1900s, the building was a hotel and gathering place for countless travelers to the rough woodsy area which became incorporated as Watkinsville in 1806. In the restoration during the 1950s, late additions to the plain plantation-style structure were eliminated to present it in its original appearance. Given the importance of the building to the area from 1789 until the 1850s or so, it should not surprise that several of spirits have apparently decided to hang around what was the epicenter of political life, commerce, and entertainment of their day.

A SKELETON IN THE CELLAR

While this building has had a rich two hundred years to attract ghosts, there is no certainty who this multitude of ghosts may be. In fact, no identity for any of the ghosts is known. However, there is some tradition regarding several of these apparitions. As to the ghost in the cellar, tradition holds that the first black man hanged in Clarke county was to die near the old courthouse, which was across the town square from the Eagle Tavern. Legend brings us no name for this wretched soul, but a rich legend surrounds his death. Prior to the man's hanging, Dr. Will Richards, the town physician, asked the gentleman if he could have his body (specifically his skeleton) for educational purposes. The man complied, and requested only that Dr. Richards provide him with all the ginger cakes he could eat between his sentence and the day of his execution (a rather strange request, but this gent apparently liked ginger cakes!). Dr. Richards was more than happy to honor that request and after the hanging, Dr. Richards claimed the body. For many years, Dr. Richards kept the skeleton as a teaching and demonstration tool for his medical practice in Watkinsville.

However, at some later point in the 1800s, Dr. Richards moved to Mississippi and, not wanting to transport the skeleton, stored it in the cellar of the Eagle Tavern. For many decades in the 1800s, this skeleton hung in the cellar, and the various owners of the building claimed that this interesting artifact was "better than burglar bars" at keeping crooks and pranksters away. Perhaps, a large black man has chosen to remain in the storage area in the cellar below the inn since his earthly remains were kept there for such a long period over a century ago.

Rekli noted that some of the sightings of spirits in the Eagle Tavern involve a large black man who apparently looks out of one of the upstairs windows. Of course, this would mean that the ghost associated with the skeleton has the run of the whole tavern, since there is no record of his skeleton having been stored in any of the upstairs rooms. However, his face has been seen in the upstairs windows by several persons over the years who were merely walking along the sidewalk in front of the Eagle Tavern.

The smell in the cellar is quite clearly a smell of dry decay—a decomposing mouse in the heating pipes might give off a similar smell, only that smell would not be limited to one small area. Again, this is one manifestation that I experienced myself in researching this story. I had gone into the basement with Rekli and smelled the odor only in that one specific, limited location in the cellar. I had a chilling thought at that moment that I was smelling one of the resident ghosts.

I should note one interesting verification of the location of the smell. As Janie is particularly afraid of the stairs and the upstairs rooms, she also noted that she would not go into the cellar by herself. In fact, she was not at work on the day that I went into the cellar on my first visit to investigate this ghost. However, I did have the opportunity to interview her two days later. Without sharing my experience with her, I asked here where in the cellar she smelled this particular apparition. She answered without hesitation, "You walk in maybe four maybe five feet, then facing the opposite wall, if I move to the left, I stepped away from the smell." When Janie described the exact location where I noted the smell in the basement, a cold shiver went down my spine, and it occurred to me that the research for this book was more than mere curiosity; this project had become a serious investigation into the unknown. Experiencing a manifestation such as this will have such an effect on anyone.

A HIDDEN SOLDIER

On the first floor of the tavern, an open fireplace for cooking and heating opens into the parlor room (the main first floor room on the south end of the building), and one spirit apparently resides in or around this chimney. Several psychics over the years have noted that this ghost prefers that particular area around the fireplace. There is some tradition as to who this ghost might be.

While the Civil War did not impact Athens in terms of major battles, there was one Union Army Raid that sent horsemen through the area in 1864. Tradition holds that a Confederate soldier remained concealed for a period of time in a hiding place in a loft behind an enormous chimney. Of course, at that time, the building was much larger and many chimneys would have been interconnected to rooms in different ways—one history reports that almost every room of the larger lodge of seventeen rooms had a different floor level from the other rooms. Many chimneys would have connected to the main chimney which is still standing, affixed to the original building from 1789. Regarding this spirit, Rekli reported, "This ghost that resides in this parlor was found by some gentlemen who claimed to be from a paranormal society that came through one weekend. They had one of those meters that shows ghostly activity and cold spot and things. Most of the activity was right there in front of the parlor fireplace."

During his period in hiding, slaves supported this soldier the length of his stay between the chimneys by handing up the narrow stairs food and buckets of hot coals for warmth. While part of the chimney behind which this confederate soldier hid was torn down with the restoration, this spirit is apparently attached to the main chimney in the parlor—perhaps his source of warmth and security during his period of fear. Various visitors have stated that they seem to hear scratching noises coming from the large remaining chimney, and that this may be a spirit seeking his freedom.

In a subsequent interview with Janie, without Rekli present, I asked her about the ghost in the parlor. We were sitting in the old general store room (the downstairs room on the north end of the building), adjacent to the parlor room. Janie replied, "Now the male spirit, or whatever it is—the presence; sometimes I feel like it's downstairs. Sometimes I feel like maybe it is standing in this doorway on the first floor between the parlor and the store. That doesn't bother me (like the female presence on the stairs)."

I asked Janie if she could sense who that ghost might be. She closed her eyes, and stated,

"A white man, young; maybe a soldier at some point. He doesn't seem lonely, and he's not bothersome."

When the remodeling was done in the early 1900s, three wagon loads of ashes were reportedly found between two of the chimneys. Perhaps a spirit, caught in the confusion of war from over a hundred and fifty years ago, is still seeking his way out.

PORTAL TO ANOTHER WORLD

A visiting physic stopped by the Eagle Tavern in 2001, and spent considerable time describing the various ghosts to Rekli. In particular that physic indicated that the well in the basement was "A portal into another dimension"— a portal to a ghostly world of spirits, and that this accounted for the unusually high ghostly activity at the tavern.

When I asked Janie about her experiences in the basement, she indicated that she wasn't sure that she believed that the old well was indeed a portal to another world. Still, she reported that when she stood over the old well, "I got this tingling sensation in my fingers." On the possibility of her staying with us on an overnight in the old tavern: "You could not pay me to stay here."

Upon reflection, perhaps we are being less than fair to the old tavern. This building has outlived any person alive today by a hundred years or more and could tell us such rich stories. Perhaps any building with that history would have a few spirits about. In fact, any old building is a portal to another world—a world of yesteryear. The Eagle Tavern stood when the rest of Big Springs (now Watkinsville) was forest and swamp, years before anyone thought of a city called

Athens. A building with the long history of this tavern has experienced lives which can be only dimly imagined by us today. Our view of the "Indian troubles" in this region of Georgia would be clouded by the inexactness of Hollywood mythmaking, and culturally biased in the extreme, but this building saw "Indian alarms" in the Big Springs community. We cannot, in any concrete sense, imagine running for our lives through the Big Springs town square towards Fort Edwards after someone shouted the alarm.

Can anyone today truly imagine five faculty members from the University of Georgia riding horses to locate a suitable spot for a seat of higher learning? How could those men have envisioned in their day the future world-wide educational leadership of the University of Georgia? How can we experience the life of the circuit riding judge staying at the tavern on court days, the sheriff's life in that small town, the dusty stage coach riders stopping over for the night and sleeping three to a bed upstairs in the old tavern? Can we envision the life of the foot travelers who, for the price of a whisky, were allowed to bunk on the parlor floor by the fire, or the hanging days when the local hangman did his ghastly work within sight of this old building? The Eagle Tavern has lived many lives, and it does transport one into another world, a bygone world of horses, of stage coaches, of simple satisfying meals at taverns, and hangings on the court-house square. This is part of the rich history preserved by this tavern, and we should not be surprised that spirits, known and unknown, attach themselves to what was, in its day, the center of life in Clarke County.

SPIRITS OF ASHFORD MANOR

A movement, perhaps a quiet swirl of wind between the manor house and the cottage, caught in the corner of one's eye, or the quick glance of a spirit drifting past an open hallway door on the second floor: such are the spirits of Ashford Manor. Located just down the street from the haunted eighteenth-century Eagle Tavern in downtown Watkinsville, Georgia, Ashford Manor appears to have many spirits; numerous different individuals have sensed spirits here and a few are quite certain that this beautiful old house, dating from just before the turn of the last century, hosts a variety of ghosts.

The well-preserved manor house on the former Ashford estate has witnessed much sad and mysterious history. The suicide of the socially prominent family patriarch, a slasher murder, and the meanderings of a headless woman dressed in blood red, lend an air of the supernatural to this exquisite house. With these occurrences over the hundred-plus-year history of the house, now renovated as a bed and breakfast, one may well expect ghosts to be frequent guests, and the spirits in this wonderful inn do not disappoint!

THE HEADLESS WOMAN IN RED

Sophie has been employed as a housekeeper at Ashford Manor since 1997 and has witnessed many strange occurrences. She is a talkative, delightful woman who was concerned that her real name not be used, her experiences be presented accurately, and that she not be presented as a "nutcase." I assured her that I was doing a serious, interview-based book on true hauntings and that I was handling each experience with fairness and respect. After a brief conversation, Sophie opened up completely and shared several examples of strange occurrences.

One afternoon, Sophie and her daughter were folding laundry on the edge of a large bed in one of the guest rooms on the second floor. They were on the same side of the bed and were chatting about various matters when both of them, at the same moment, turned suddenly to their left. Someone had soundlessly walked down the hallway past the bedroom door. Sophie recalled that the apparition seemed to be a woman in a blood-red dress, and that she seemed to be walking along noiselessly, even gliding. Most frightening, she appeared to have no head! As the two women saw this, they quickly looked back at each other, and Sophie's daughter silently mouthed the words "Did you see that?" Sophie—again without making a sound—answered "Yes.". Sophie then went to the door, and looked into the hallway, fully expecting—if not dreading—to see this same horrifying vision; but no one was there. Sophie remains nonetheless certain from that first moment that she and her daughter had both seen a spirit. She reported that she was not really frightened, but wanted to know what she had seen. More than anything else, she was curious as to what this phenomenon might be.

Sophie reports that on numerous other occasions she has sensed a presence in various rooms of the house. In each case this spirit has appeared silently, and generally it was just an uneasy sensation that she is not alone. Most of her experiences have involved spirits passing by doorways leading into the second-floor hallway. Of course, with her job responsibilities, one may well expect that she would spend much of her time in the second-floor guest rooms. While Sophie has lived in the Watkinsville area all of her life, she has no knowledge of local lore which would explain who this headless woman in red may be.

HISTORY OF THE HOUSE

Alexander Woodson Ashford built his first home on these acres in 1878, and that house, now referred to as the cottage, is where the current owners live. In 1893, Ashford built a larger residence to house his wife and nine children, and it is this structure which serves as an inn today.. These houses on Harden Hill Road remained in the same family for over a hundred years, and only passed into outside hands a few years ago.

David Shearon and Mario Castro are the current owners of the home. They bought the house from Ashford descendants in 1997 specifically for renovating as a bed and breakfast. While these gentlemen were by no means looking for a haunted house, it didn't take long for them to discover their other-worldly visitors.

Shearon and Castro actually experienced their first haunted experience one day before they bought the house, on May 31, 1997. With the owners' permission, they were staying in the house the evening before they closed on the purchase of the house. Shearon and Castro were staying in a bedroom on the second floor, and were awakened by a loud crash from the floor below. They ran downstairs to investigate and ascertained that no one was in the building (indeed, no one but themselves was supposed to be!) and, without finding the source of the noise, they eventually went back to sleep.

The next morning as they were going to the closing, they noticed that one arm of a large brass chandelier in a downstairs room had broken and dropped a crystal globe to the floor. This accounted for the crash of the night before; the broken globe was obvious in the daylight. Originally, A. W. Ashford, the first owner of the home, had used that particular room with this wonderful chandelier on the north side of the main floor as his bedroom. Originally a gasolier, this hundred-year-old metal fixture was reworked early in the twentieth century for electricity. At the time, these gentlemen thought nothing of the broken fixture, since some work was being done on the house. However, at the closing, the former owners assured them that the chandelier in question had just been repaired and that all of the joints in the brass support arms had been securely re-soldered specifically to prevent this type of weakness in the light fixture! Why would a newly secured brass joint have given way?

WHO THESE SPIRITS MIGHT BE

Shearon and Castro indicate that they really had very little idea who the spirits in the old house might be. They state that most of their uneasy feelings stem from glimpses of mysterious shadows in the yard between the cottage and the manor house. On many occasions they have felt that they saw a presence move from one building to the other, but they have no idea who the spirits could be. But the innkeepers do know that over the last century at least three deaths have occurred in the house or on the estate.

A. W. Ashford, the builder of the manor house, was a prominent banker and suffered a major financial loss in the Great Crash of 1929. Distraught, he ended his own life at a bank only a few blocks away, and legend suggests that his body was prepared for burial and placed in the main floor room that served as his bedroom. Perhaps his spirit still wanders Ashford Manor. (After Ashford's death, his son John used the same room as his bedroom for years thereafter, and his spirit likewise may still drift over these grounds.)

There is also a local legend of a murder victim who had his throat brutally slashed and was left for dead near a creek on the back of the property. He is believed to have died in the same north-facing bedroom as a result of his injuries.   Today, this room serves as the dining area for bed and breakfast guests, and the fabled chandelier is under repair yet again. The owners have no clue who the spirit of the woman in red may be.

THE EVIDENCE FOR THIS HAUNTING

It is always more compelling to find an incident of haunting that involves a number of witnesses. In this case, three separate, credible witnesses who had, over the years since 1997, experienced an array of strange occurrences came forth with their stories. Further, these witnesses were neither hysterically frightened by the phenomenon they witnesses, nor totally enthralled with them. In fact, each exhibited a healthy dose of skepticism, lending more credence to their accounts.

Neither Shearon nor Castro are sure that they have actually experienced a haunting. In going public about what they have seen, they are not sure if such experiences would be bad or good for business, and thus seem to have no real incentive to invent their tales.

Sophie, on the other hand, does believe in spirits and is convinced that several inhabit the old manor house. While she has never reported abject fear, she is respectful of these occurrences and usually watches the upstairs hallway closely. While most of Sophie's experiences involve sightings inside the home, most of the owners' experiences involve faint images or glimpses of forms moving across the yard from the cottage to the manor house. Interestingly, all three report that their strange experiences have been declining over the years; that is, when the house was first reworked as a bed and breakfast, many sightings were reported, but more recently, the spirits seemed to be a bit active.

A visit to the Ashford Manor Bed and Breakfast is certainly warranted, and perhaps if you look carefully, you may yet see a hint of an apparition moving down the second-floor hallway or across the lawn toward the cottage. But here we leave the spirits of Ashford Manor—uncertain as to who they may be, and unsure how to investigate further. Still, with the declining appearances of these apparitions, perhaps it is for the best that we investigate no more. If these spirits have found their peace, let us trouble them no further.

A PRIMER OF ATLANTA AND
NORTH GEORGIA GHOSTS

What do we know about ghosts in Atlanta and north Georgia? For that matter, what do we know about ghosts in general? In spite of the work represented in this book, not to mention the hundreds of other studies, research projects, and books, the answer to what we know can still be summed up in two words: *absolutely nothing.*

Of course, stating this conclusion so blatantly may offend some readers, some believers in ghosts, and ghost hunters, but the plain fact is we do not know if ghosts exist, much less what physical laws govern their appearances, why they come to us, or how they manifest themselves. Some believe that photographs in ghostly graveyards which reveal strange "orbs" or circular shapes represent spirits, and indeed, some of these orbs *do* seem to move across the camera's field of view. There are many websites which post various photographs of this nature. In particular, the Georgia Haunt Hunt Team site, www.geocities.com/gahaunt, has several ghostly photographs of the Kennesaw Battlefield and the Old Athens Cemetery which are quite interesting.

Others ghost researchers suggest that ghosts impact the physical environment with temperature changes, and a common refrain among those who have experienced an apparation is something to the effect that "It suddenly grew colder, in that corner of the room. . . ." Several people interviewed for this book, including Shay Virtue at the Wedding Cake House, have had that experience. These temperature differences are the reason that many ghost hunters use heat detection devices or photography in the infrared spectrum to demonstrate the existence of ghosts. Cheri Mohr Drake of the Georgia Haunt Hunt Team indicated that her team has recorded a fifty degree temperature difference within a two-inch distance in the middle of the Old Athens Cemetery on Jackson Street.

Perhaps over time these more scientific approaches to the documentation of ghosts will bear fruit. However, in spite of these approaches, there is today not a single fact or theory which is widely accepted by the general scientific community about ghosts, including their very existence. Thus, I have to state that from a purely scientific point of view, the existence of ghosts cannot be proven.

WHAT SHOULD ONE CONSIDER
EVIDENCE OF A GHOST?

Still, what does one mean by *proof* in this context? Further, who sets the criteria for proof? In today's world, nothing becomes accepted by science until and unless

1. there is proof of the relevant facts, using scientifically accepted and repeatable methodologies, and
2. someone has provided an underlying theory to explain or provide a context for the proven fact or facts.

In the study of ghosts, neither of these components of proof were present as of the writing of this book. However, there is some anecdotal evidence—which I find to be intriguing and persuasive—which can be presented relative to each of these Atlanta and north Georgia ghost stories. Further, I want to describe what I consider evidence of ghosts.

When I begin to investigate a ghost story, I try whenever possible to talk with a number of people who have experienced the same ghost or manifestation, in order to get a broad picture of the appearance and nature of the apparition or manifestation. In short, two or more viewers are always preferable to only one, and three are preferable to two. Whenever possible, I have interviewed a variety of people who have experienced the strange manifestation, or I have reviewed earlier credible reports of these ghostly manifestations. These Atlanta stories vary considerably in terms of who and how many persons I could interview—in this regard, the stories speak for themselves. With their permission, I have noted the names of interviewees, as well as examples of manifestations that I obtained from other reports through hearsay evidence.

Next, I always want to make some judgments about the "normalcy" or emotional condition of the observers of the ghost prior to determining my level of belief that a ghost is present. A manifestation experience gains credibility, in my view, when the person having the experience is something of a skeptic on supernatural phenomenon. In point of fact, I often heard from people who had experienced these manifestations a protestation that, "I didn't believe in ghosts until . . . ," or "I'm not sure this was a ghost, but. . . ." This increases my confidence that the person is, at least, reporting something unexplainable. I've noted in these stories my sense of the complete reliability of these witnesses as to their hauntings. I have not included in this book any stories or interviews from individuals who I considered not credible—all of these reported interviewees were quite convincing in their description of what they experienced. These interviewees were all very sincere, many were very accomplished individuals, holding very responsible positions in society, and functioning quite successfully in life. They were completely, and without exception, believable—they saw or experienced exactly what they described, in my judgment, and while neither I nor they can explain in scientific terms what they experienced, I and they consider these hauntings true in every sense of that word.

Many "ghost story" books leave one quite unhappy; many such books present the ghost story from only one person's perspective, and do not discuss research methodology and the sources for the stories. Herein, I've tried to provide some context and history for each story. This is what I prefer in ghost stories, and what I consider to be a valid, though preliminary, exploration into an unknown yet real phenomenon. Moreover, I hope this results in accounts of true ghost stories that are more satisfying for the reader.

Next, I want to follow the story through, cradle to grave or beginning to end, as it were. More often than not, such investigative follow-through is not possible. However, when possible, I've tried to provide historical evidence of the actual story, as well as note the location of the graves of the apparitions, if at all possible. I investigated the Civil War battles of Kennesaw Mountain, Peachtree Creek, Atlanta, and Stone Mountain village. I was able to locate the graves of Captain Peeler, Linton Harris, and General Robert Toombs, though I couldn't find a grave for Susie Carithers of the Wedding Cake House. I visited every possible site mentioned in this book, for example, I did stand in Oakland Cemetery by the Lion of Atlanta where the "Roll Call of the Dead" has been heard.

For me, when I visit the grave site of, say, Captain Hiram Peeler, whose supernatural presence is described in "Captain Peeler's Fire Hall," I experience a sense of completion of the story. I stood by Captain Peeler's grave one Sunday evening at dusk; I knew and experienced him as a real man, in the context of the late-nineteenth and early-twentieth century, a man with a family, a man of dreams and ambition. He worked hard in his chosen profession, and died doing his duty for his community. Standing by his grave not only brought home a profound respect for the captain, but cemented the context of his story for me. A man lived, made a contribution to his world, lead other men in making the world safe for others, and then died in service. I needed to see the captain's grave in the Oconee Hill Cemetery, and to contemplate in my mind's eye a gathering of people around that grave in 1928, perhaps a parent, wife, children, or siblings.

These then, have been my goals; not only to write an interesting book on local ghosts in Atlanta and beyond, but to place each tale in context and to explore the believability of each event. Depending upon the story, I believe that I succeeded in varying degrees.

THEORIES OF SPIRITS

What then is a ghost? Of the many competing theories, three in particular stand out. First, the belief that ghosts are disincarnate spirits of dead human beings (and perhaps even animals) is by far the most common theory. Some believe ghosts have unfinished business, while others think ghosts may be ignorant for some reason on where they should go after death. Those who hold this theory simply don't know.

Another view is that ghosts result, not from the spirit of the deceased, but from the need of the living, that currently living individuals somehow call ghosts into existence. This theory that persons who see spirits may consciously or unconsciously "create" them out of some unfulfilled psychological need is more complex that it at first appears, however. Given this idea, some might suggest that these people would be better advised to spend their money with a good psychologist than describing the apparition which they think they saw. However, this is a very elementary and belittling view of this perspective.

A more enlightened view of the living-persons-creating-ghosts theory involves the realization that ideas are creative forces, in and of themselves. We create because we first envision. Using Biblical eschatology, God indeed created the universe with his word alone. Can the mind of mankind do the same? Under this view, perhaps someone can imagine a spirit or ghost, and that creative act alone can result in some "call" and result in the existence of a spiritual energy—a ghost.

A third theory of what a ghost is involves the interaction of the other theories highlighted above, i.e. that disincarnate spirits exist independent of living humans and that it takes some conscious or unconscious will on the part of a living human being to "call" the spirit back into this universe. Perhaps both are necessary for a ghostly manifestation.

Personally, as a student of psychology, I would like to accept the third theory, because in human dynamics almost everything is interactive. However, upon reflection, I cannot accept this view. Simply stated, there are too many instances in which persons were not consciously thinking of a spirit at all but nevertheless saw one. At present, I have to lean toward the first theory above—that ghosts are rare examples of disincarnate spirits that exist independently of the human consciousness of living individuals.

THEN WHAT DO WE THINK WE KNOW?

As for what we know about ghosts, many who take the study of ghosts seriously would suggest that we *do* know certain things. While no ironclad proof of these propositions is available, we think we know that

1. Ghosts or apparitions are extremely rare. While millions of persons have lived in Atlanta and north Georgia from its Native American history to the present day, only a few of these spirits resulted in ghostly manifestations. One may only assume that most of us do indeed know where to go after death, or we are somehow lead.
2. Ghosts typically do not seem to result from the normal processes of living and dying. Instead, many seem to have met untimely or tragic deaths; suicide or violent accidents, for example, would certainly qualify. Some have suggested that ghosts may be spirits who have not yet realized they are dead, or who may have unfinished business on the earthly plain. In very many cases, tragic love or painful and

quick death do seem to be part and parcel of ghost stories.

3. Ghost stories, in total, seem to suggest that ghosts can become attached to objects, buildings, or locations which were meaningful in their life. There seem to be many more ghosts in buildings that played a role in life, as opposed to cemeteries, for example. In fact, when one considers the comparison between one's home and a family cemetery, where does one spend the most time while alive? Attachment to particular objects is also quite common, and almost every Atlanta ghost seems attached to a building or other location.

4. Most ghosts manifest themselves in only two or three different ways. For example, a ghost may manifest the sound of dragging a chair across a floor, if they did so prior to hanging, or appear in a uniform, if they died during military service. It is interesting to note that spooks apparently have two to three ways to manifest, and most seem to be limited to only a few actions. One rarely finds ghosts that are known to do more that two or three types of manifestations, regardless of the multi-functioning "poltergeist" theme often depicted by Hollywood.

5. Many ghosts seem to have a mission to help those alive in some way. One can often hear of ghosts that warn the living about impending doom. The Ghost of Midtown seems to have this type of mild disposition and the ghost of Sally Carithers in the sorority house in Athens does appear to assist young women in getting engaged, but those are the rare exceptions in these stories. It is interesting to note that not many of the ghosts in Atlanta or north Georgia appear to have such intentions or any particular mission.

6. When a ghost appears not to have a particular mission, accounts of it usually reveal a fairly benign spirit, with no apparent intention to scare the living. Indeed, regardless of the use of ghost stories on Halloween to scare children and adults alike, finding a ghost who consistently manifests ill intentions is quite rare. Elizabeth, when experiencing the Ghost of Midtown, noted a feeling of well-being rather that fright, as did her roommate Julie. Similarly, Lee Knipperberg felt no fear in her experience of the ghost of Wendell Brown at

Oglethorpe University. Rather than menacing, these spirits seemed protective in some way.

7. Many ghosts seem somewhat confused, or even unaware of what is happening to them. In the Ghost in Midtown story, the eyewitness indicated that the ghost seemed surprised when she saw him and spoke to him. This type of occurrence has lead to the oft-repeated theme that ghosts are "lost souls" who never "went beyond." Of course, with the expected skepticism, one wants to inquire "beyond to where?" The answer to that question, as near as I can determine, is unknown.

8. Ghosts seem to manifest themselves when their environs are upset in some way. Mohr Drake suggests that ghostly manifestations are much more likely to occur during or after a renovation of a property to which a ghost is emotionally attached, and that theme is common in these experiences in Atlanta. Renovations seem to upset the spirit somehow, and the ghost may function as if the renovation had not taken place; for example, when a wall blocks an earlier entrance, the ghost may appear to walk through the new wall. Thus, one would expect more appearances of the ghost of Sally Carithers if and when the Wedding Cake House receives a periodic painting or general facelift.

A CONCLUSION AND A BEGINNING

As this relatively short list shows, we know nothing about ghosts beyond a scientific doubt, and even with a liberal dose of faith, when it comes to ghosts, we still know very little. These points are not very solid at all, and clearly there is a great deal of work to be done in this field. Nevertheless, logical inquiry into any phenomenon must begin somewhere, and around the world, numerous researchers are beginning to seriously consider these and other manifestations as representing something that we don't understand, as opposed to something we should continue to choose to ignore. That distinction, as minute as it may seem, sews the seed of new understandings of, and perhaps new tolerance for, all forms of "life."

Electricity, although observable in natural phenomenon such as lightning, the aurora borealis, and static electricity, went unexplained for hundreds of thousands of years of human prehistory and approximately ten thousand years of civilization. It was only a little more than two hundred and fifty years ago that Benjamin Franklin—with his famous kite-and-key experiment—"discovered" that lightning and electricity are the same and proved that lightning is an electrical current in nature. This seems incredible when we consider how much we have harnessed this power in today's world. Still, such is the result of the unchallenged stupidity of ignoring real phenomenons experienced by honest observers each and every day.

I cannot tell the reader what a ghost is, but I can assure the reader that ghosts exist. Further, the next century will explore this venue of consciousness thoroughly. Perhaps then humankind will progress a bit more—one can only hope.

Thus, my wish for the inquisitive, open-minded reader is that he or she will practice the suspended disbelief described earlier in this book, explore all the possibilities, and find that position as powerful as I have. Perhaps that position—and this compilation of true Atlanta and north Georgia hauntings—can assist in moving our understanding forward.

REFERENCES

Allen, Judy. "The Believers." *Atlanta*, 9 (3, 1969): 53–54.

Athens (Georgia) *Banner Herald*, Athens, Ga.: Athens Banner Herald, 1928–2002.

Atlanta Journal Constitution Atlanta: Atlanta Journal Constitution, 1995–2001.

Bodine, Echo L. *Relax, It's Only a Ghost: My Adventures with Spirits, Hauntings, and Things that Go Bump in the Night.* Boston: Fair Winds Press, 2001.

Bickley, R. Bruce. *Joel Chandler Harris.* Athens, Ga.: University of Georgia Press, 1987.

Boney, F. N. *A Pictorial History of the University of Georgia.* Athens, Ga.: University of Georgia Press, 1984.

Coffey, David A. *John Bell Hood and the Struggle for Atlanta.* Abilene, Texas: McWhiney Foundation Press, 1998.

Duffey, G. *Angels and Apparitions: True Ghost Stories from the South.* Eatonton, Ga.: Elysian Publishing Company, 1996.

DeBolt, M. W. *Savannah Specters and Other Strange Tales.* Virginia Beach, Va.: Donning Company, 1984.

Denning, H. M. *True Hauntings: Spirits With A Purpose.* St. Paul, Minn.; Llewellyn Publications, 1999.

Egan, A. "Georgia Ghosts: From Cemeteries to Civil War Battlefields, Learn about Southern Spirits." *Points North* October, 2000.

Goodman, M. "Friendly Spirits Share Historic Farmhouse." *Points North* October 2001.

Hauck, Dennis William. *Haunted Places: The National Directory. A Guidebook to Ghostly Abodes, Sacred Sites, UFO Landings and Other Supernatural Locations.* New York: Penguin Books, 2002.

Heys, Sam, and Allen B. Goodwin. *The Winecoff Fire : The Untold Story of America's Deadliest Hotel Fire.* Atlanta: Longstreet Press, 1993.

Hull, Augustus Longstreet, ed. *Annals of Athens, Georgia, 1801–1901.* Danielsville, Ga.: Heritage Papers, 1978.

Kelly, D. *Kennesaw Mountain and the Atlanta Campaign: A Tour Guide.*
Atlanta: Susan Hunter Publishing, 1999.

Monroe, Robert A. *Journeys Out of the Body.* New York: Main Street
Books/Doubleday, 1973.

Morris, S. "Athens and Clarke County." In *History of Athens and Clarke
County,* edited by D. C. Barrow. New York: H. J. Rowe, 1923

Myers, Arthur. *The Ghostly Register* New York: Contemporary Books Inc.,
1986.

Price, V. "The Ghost & Mr. Kitchens." *The Times of DeKalb* published by the
DeKalb Historical Society, Atlanta, 1995 February: 3.

Rich, J. *The Everything Ghost Book.* Avon, Mass.: Adams Media Corporation,
2001.

Roberts, N. *Georgia Ghosts.* Winston-Salem, N.C.: John F. Blair, 1997.

Rose, Michael. *Atlanta: A Portrait of the Civil War.* Atlanta: Atlanta History
Center.

Smith, Adam. *Powers of Mind.* New York: Summit Books, 1982.

Tate, Susan Frances Barrow. *Remembering Athens.* Athens, Ga.: Athens Historical Society, 1996.

Tate, William. *Strolls Around Athens.* Athens, Ga.: Observer Press, 1975.

The Ultimate Ten Unsolved Mysteries. The Learning Channel, 2002.

Windham, Karen Tucker. *13 Georgia Ghosts and Jeffrey.* Tuscaloosa, Ala.: University of Alabama Press, 1973.